PRAYER PLATOON:

A Small Group Study of Prayer Warfare

Rev. Dr. William L. Hernandez

For my eight arrows who are also my eight treasures.

Thank you to my helper, my bride, for your proofreading and suggestions.

Thank you to Pastor Jesse for your insights into what can hinder our prayers.

Contents

PRAYER PLATOON DISCUSSION 1: 6

Defining Prayer 7

Find Your Prayer Partners 8

Opposition to Your Prayer Life...................................9

Layout of This Prayer Journal...................................12

DAILY PRAYERS...15

~Morning 1~ 16

Introduction to Prayer Battleground One: The
Fellowship of Loving Others.....................................16

Relational Vision & Strategy 1 ~ Spouse 21

Green, Yellow, and Red Weeks 23

~Morning 2~...24

Level Zero Groups: Afghanistan - Brazil 28

~Morning 3~ 31

Relational Vision & Strategy 2 ~ Children 34

~Morning 4~...36

Level Zero Groups: Brazil – Burkina Faso 39

~Morning 5~ 42

The Fellowship of Loving Others...........................42

Relational Vision & Strategy 3 ~ Parents 45

~Morning 6~ 47

The Fellowship of Loving Others...........................47

Level Zero Groups: Burundi – Chad 50

~Morning 7~ 53

Relational Vision & Strategy 4 ~ Distressed
Neighbors/Poor..56

PRAYER PLATOON DISCUSSION 2: Part I. Review the War
Plan for Loving Others..58

Part II. Introduction to Prayer Battleground Two: The
Fellowship of Listening to Christ 60

~Morning 8~ 62

Level Zero Groups: Chad – China 65

~Morning 9~ 68

Relational Vision & Strategy 5 ~ Hospitality to
Outsiders..71

~Morning 10~ 73

Level Zero Groups: China – Congo, DRC 76

~Morning 11~ 79

Relational Vision & Strategy 6 ~ Temple
Maintenance 82

~Morning 12~ 84

Level Zero Groups: Congo, DRC – Gabon..............87

~Morning 13~..90

Relational Vision & Strategy 7 ~ Leaning on Christ
....93

~Morning 14~ 96

Level Zero Groups: Gabon - Iran 99

PRAYER PLATOON DISCUSSION 3: Part I. Review the War Plan for Listening to our Beloved Savior and King 102

Part II. Introduction to Prayer Battleground Three: The Fellowship of Praise 104

Introduction: The Warfare Against Thanksgiving ...104

~Morning 15~ 106

Relational Vision & Strategy 8 ~ Leaning on Christ with Others 109

~Morning 16~ 111

Level Zero Groups: Iran – Laos............................114

~Morning 17~ 117

Relational Vision & Strategy 9 ~ Fasting 120

~Morning 18~ 122

Level Zero Groups: Laos – Malaysia....................125

~Morning 19~ 128

Relational Vision & Strategy 10 ~ Listening to Christ 131

~Morning 20~ 133

Level Zero Groups: Maldives – New Caledonia...136

~Morning 21~ 139

Relational Vision & Strategy 11 ~ Sharing Christ with Others 142

PRAYER PLATOON DISCUSSION 4: Part I. Review the War Plan for Praising our Beloved Savior and King 144

Part II. Introduction to Prayer Battleground Four: The Fellowship of Leaning on our Beloved Savior and King 146

Introduction: The Warfare Against Leaning on our Beloved Savior and King 146

~Morning 22~ 148

Level Zero Groups: New Caledonia – Russia 151

~Morning 23~..154

Relational Vision & Strategy 12 ~ Thanksgiving ..157

~Morning 24~ 159

Level Zero Groups: Russia – Sudan 162

~Morning 25~..165

Relational Vision & Strategy 13 ~ Worshiping God Together 168

~Morning 26~..170

Level Zero Groups: Sudan – Tanzania 173

~Morning 27~..176

Relational Vision & Strategy 14 ~ "Add lavishly to your faith heroic deeds…" (2 Peter 1:5a) 179

~Morning 28~..181

Level Zero Groups: Tanzania – Zambia 184

PRAYER PLATOON DISCUSSION 5: Part I. Review the War Plan for Leaning on our Beloved Savior and King 188

Part II. Continue in Your Prayer Platoon or Start Another Prayer Platoon. 190

~Morning 29~ 191

Scripture Reading Plan 191

~Morning 30~ 195

Practice Sharing the Gospel 195

About the author: 199

PRAYER PLATOON DISCUSSION 1:

1) On a scale of 1 to 10, with 10 being the highest, how consistent and fervent is your prayer life?

_____

_____

_____

Memory Verse:
"Persevere in prayer, being vigilant in it with thanksgiving"
(Colossians 4:2, MOUNCE).

Introduction
Platoon: A group of soldiers that includes two or more squads usually led by one lieutenant (Merriam-Webster)

My opponent thrust the wooden knife toward my abdomen. I deflected the attack. Then, we repeated the exercise. This was a part of my training in jujitsu with 25 other students at the dojo (martial arts training center) that stood near the edge of my hometown.

In the same way that I, *with a group*, learned jujitsu, the Scriptures teach us how to be on guard *together* against the attacks of the evil one. God desires for you to be in a *spiritual platoon* that has Christ as its commander. God desires for you to be protected from our spiritual enemy's attacks. The attacks of the enemy center on one thing: Destroying your prayer life and the prayer lives of other Believers.

Defining Prayer

2) How do you define prayer?

_____

_____

_____

One of the words for prayer in Hebrew, *Pagha*, can be translated, "a meeting with an outcome." Moses met with God (See **Isaiah 64:3-5**). God revealed Himself to Moses as **"I AM"** (Heb. *Yahweh*) in **Exodus 3:14**, which emphasized His eternal nature. Jesus used the phrase, "I AM" in reference to Himself in the Gospels. These "I AM" statements are quoted in this study to focus our attention on our "meetings" with the Lord.

Christ stated in some of His final words to the Disciples, **"...and lo, I am with you always, even to the end of the age" (Matthew 28:20b, NASB 1977)**. In the Greek text, the flow of thought is, **"I—with you—AM"**.

Thus, the "I AM" statements of Christ highlight the essence of our prayer life, our "fellowship" with God.

3) When do you feel closest to God? How do you meet with God?

_____

_____

_____

An operational definition for prayer can be:

$$R\ (A + Y)^{S}:$$

i. **R**esting in His presence, **"casting all your anxiety on Him, because He cares for you" (1 Peter 5:7, NASB)**,
ii. **A**ppreciation of Him,
iii. **Y**oke with Christ of love toward others, and
iv. **S**itting at His feet to listen to His teaching.

These four branches of prayer become the four battlegrounds in prayer warfare. Take time every evening to reflect on how you did in these areas. As you meet with your Prayer Platoon, you can review how you are doing in these four areas.

Find Your Prayer Partners
4) With whom do your pray?

_____

_____

_____

Our prayer life is never based solely on our own efforts. Our "meeting" with the Lord is done in "fellowship" (*Koinonia*) with the Holy Spirit, who is called our "Helper" (*Parakletos*). One of the meanings of fellowship is "joint participation". Of our fellowship with the Spirit it is written, **"May the grace of the Lord Jesus Christ, and the love of God, and the fellowship [joint participation] of the Holy Spirit be with you all" (1 Corinthians 13:14, NIV).** The Holy Spirit was given to us as a "Helper". It is written, **"But the Helper, the Holy Spirit, whom the Father will send in my name, he will teach you all things and bring to your remembrance all that I have said to you" (John 14:26, ESV).** Thus, we will highlight in this study the various ways the Holy Spirit fellowships with us, coming along side us to help us on the battlegrounds of prayer warfare. **"Then he replied, "This is the word the LORD spoke to Zerubbabel: You won't [succeed] by might or by power, but by my Spirit, says the LORD of Armies" (Zechariah 4:6, GWT).** Our fellowship is also with one another and with the Father and the Son **(1 Corinthians 13:14; 1 John 1:3)**.

Opposition to Your Prayer Life

5) Why do you think prayer is so hard?

_____

_____

_____

Jesus the Messiah taught, **"I am the vine; you are the branches. If you remain in me and I in you, you will** bear much fruit; apart from me you can do nothing" **(John 15:5, NIV)**. The promise of bearing fruit is seeing others come to faith **(Romans 1:13)**. We focus on abiding in Christ that we can **"bear much fruit" (John 15:5a, NIV)**. This is a true promise from our Lord. He also says, **"apart from me you can do nothing (John 15:5b, NIV)**. So, if you want a bunch of **"nothing"**, neglect your prayer life and you will get it! Let's stay **"vigilant"** in prayer together **(Colossians 4:2)**. Let's be obsessed with prayer!

6) On a scale of 1 to 10, with 10 being the highest, how much does your church pray for missions?

_____

_____

_____

Christ taught us to bear fruit among the nations. He said, **"And this gospel of the kingdom will be preached in the whole world as a testimony to all nations, and then the end will come" (Matthew 24:14, NIV)**. When the end comes, it will be "game over" for the enemy. He has nothing to look forward to except a lake of fire **(Revelation 20:10)**. The enemy is doing everything he can to try to postpone his coming destruction.

If I were on the enemy's team, I would do everything to hinder the Gospel from getting to the last reached groups on earth. There is a verse that states, **"...Satan blocked the way" (1 Thessalonians 2:18b, NIV)**. The meaning of the Greek word translated, "blocked", is that of an army in retreat which, "breaks up the road", thus hindering the pursuing army – hindering. That is what Satan is trying to do – *hinder your platoon*. But we will pursue. The Good News of God's forgiveness and new life will reach the last reached groups **(Revelation 5:9)**, even at great sacrifice. These groups deserve to hear the hope of salvation as much as you or I did. We will bear fruit among them. Our Lord taught, **"This kind of spirit can be forced out only by prayer," (Mark 9:29, GWT)**. As we reach the last of the last, Jesus' teaching must be taken seriously.

As we go forward *as a prayer platoon*, bringing the message of God's forgiveness and new life to the last of the last people groups on earth, that is, to **"all nations" (Matthew 24:14, NIV)**, there will be an increase in international conflict, **"…wars and rumors of wars" (Matthew 24:6, NIV)**. I am persuaded that this is an attempt to block God's workers from getting access to countries which house the last groups to be reached on earth. I am also persuaded (and have experienced) that there will be an increased level of personal attacks against God's workers and those who help them. These attacks focus on destroying our prayer lives.

To be **truly** willing to pray at all costs, to **truly** persevere in prayer, and **truly** seek only victory in our prayer lives so that the Gospel goes forward to all nations is to put on **"the belt of truth" (Ephesians 6:14, NIV)**, which keeps us from being hindered by the "loose ends" of the clothing of unwillingness in warfare.[1] For

---

[1] John MacArthur, ed., *The MacArthur Study Bible* (Nashville: Thomas Nelson Publishers, 1997), note on Ephesians 6:14.

those who are willing, I welcome you to the battlefield
of prayer warfare. I welcome you to vigilantly meet with
God and bear fruit among the nations.

Layout of This Prayer Journal

    7)   What are some obstacles that would keep you
from going through this study over the next
four weeks?

_____

_____

_____

The following pages are arranged as a monthly
devotional to keep us vigilant about defending our
prayer lives throughout the month.

- The "Daily Prayers" page is for listing those
  closest to you, your spiritual children, and
  people groups closest to your heart.
- Following the "Daily Prayers" page, there is a
  30-day devotional. Each day begins with some
  verses that highlight what may hinder your
  prayers. There are about sixty ways that our
  prayers can be hindered according to the
  Scriptures. As we think through these verses
  daily, let us be mindful with the Apostle Paul,
  who said, **"I don't want Satan to outwit us.
  After all, we are not ignorant about Satan's
  scheming (2 Corinthians 2:11, GWT)**. As you
  work through this manual month after month,
  may prayer and defending your prayer life

become as natural and consistent for you as breathing.

- There are five "Prayer Platoon Discussion" sections (including this one) for guiding this four-week study.
- Each day also has a page for listing believers and non-believers for whom you are praying. This is also good to remind you to be in touch with those you've listed.
- Every other day of the devotional there are relationships listed. Reflect on these vital relationships and journal your vision and strategies for maintaining these relationships. Reflect on your goals, struggles, and successes in these relationships.
- There are listed on every other day of the devotional the last people groups on earth to be reached with the Gospel. These are the most desperate to hear of the hope we have. If you are praying in a group, the leader and group can alternate praying for every other people group. Pray for these groups that God will send them missionaries and that He would prepare their hearts to receive the message of hope.
- On "Day 28" there is a place to write down notes during fasting, "Juice Day Notes." Use this page when you fast. Write down the thoughts God leads you to ponder.

An operational definition of joy is to know your purpose and to live it. You were designed to be a part of a Prayer Platoon. There is no greater joy than meeting with God, defending your prayer life, and seeing others come to faith **(Acts 2:28)**.

Our prayer is that this study will be a useful tool that gets into the hands of the most strategic of God's people who will fellowship with God in bringing the Gospel to all nations. Our most strategic realm is in encouraging, teaching, and equipping the Body of Christ to pray.

*   *   *

~ DAILY PRAYERS ~

Prayer is a relationship of love

Lord Jesus, we desire Your presence. You promised, "and lo, I am with you always, even to the end of the age" (Matt. 28:20b, NASB).

Turn to Jesus through the "I AM" statements!

"I tell you the truth, before Abraham was even born, I AM!" (John 8:58, NLT).

1) Household & Spiritual Children

-
-
-
-
-
-
-
-
-
-
-
-

2) People groups

-
-

~Morning 1~

Introduction to Prayer Battleground One: *The Fellowship of Loving Others*

1) On a scale of 1 to 10, with 10 being the highest, how much do your minister to others in your own strength?

_____

_____

_____

Memory Verse

"Come to me, all you who are weary and burdened, and I will give you rest. Take my yoke upon you and learn from me for I am meek and lowly in heart and you will find rest for your souls, for my yoke is easy and my burden is light" (Matthew 11:28-29, NIV).

Introduction: The Warfare Against Relationships

2) Do you perceive that the way you treat others is the way you are treating Christ himself?

_____

_____

_____

Jesus the Messiah always loved others. We serve "yoked" with Him. We never serve alone. Christ taught, **"…whatever you did for the least of these brothers and sisters of mine, you did for me" (Matthew 25:40).** Thus, Christ helps us to love others. Christ accepts your love or lack of love toward others as your love or lack of love toward Him. In addition, the Spirit of God helps us to serve others, as it is written, **"…we serve in the new way of the Spirit, and not in the old way of the written code" (Romans 6:7b, NIV).**

3) In what relationships do you struggle the most in terms of serving and speaking in love?

_____

_____

_____

Satan, in order to block your way from abiding in Christ, desires to keep you in <u>bondage to hatred and neglect in your relationships</u>, that you might not bear fruit. Some of the following verses illustrate bondage to <u>forms of hatred and neglect in our relationships</u>, which hinder our prayers. Others of the following verses demonstrate how to abide in Christ through vigilantly serving others. Take time to reflect on these verses daily so that you can defend your prayer life.

The Fellowship of Loving Others

Lord, help us defend our prayer lives, for our fellowship with You is hindered by...

1. Dishonoring one's spouse
    - "In the same way, you husbands must give honor to your wives. Treat your wife with understanding as you live together. She may be weaker than you are, but she is your equal partner in God's gift of new life. Treat her as you should so your prayers will not be hindered" (1 Peter 3:7, NLT).
    - "Those who consider themselves religious and yet do not keep a tight rein on their tongues deceive themselves, and their religion is worthless" (James 1:26, NIV).
    - [Speaking of Christ, it was written,] "He will not shout or cry out, or raise his voice in the streets" (Isaiah 42:2, NIV).
    - "And if a woman has a husband who is not a believer and he is willing to live with her, she must not divorce him" (1 Corinthians 7:13, NIV).

Not praying with our families

- "Pour out your wrath...on the families that do not call Your name..." (Jeremiah 10:25a, NASB).

How do these verses describe fellowship with darkness or fellowship with God?

_____

_____

_____

_____

_____

_____

_____

Talk to God about your struggles in these areas.

_____

_____

_____

_____

_____

_____

Seek strength from God to fellowship with Him. **"If anyone serves, they should do so with the strength God provides, so that in all things God may be praised through Jesus Christ. To him be the glory and the power for ever and ever. Amen" (1 Peter 4:11b, NIV).**

_____

_____

_____

_____

_____

Jesus, we draw near to You. You said,

"I am the bread of life. Whoever comes to me will never be hungry again. Whoever believes in me will never be thirsty" (John 6:35, NLT).

1) Daily prayers & prayer for today's schedule

2) Believers *(Names beginning with the letter 'A')*

-
-
-
-
-
-
-
-
-

3) Unbelievers & People Groups

-
-
-
-
-
-
-

Relational Vision & Strategy 1 ~ Spouse

What are your goals, struggles, and successes in this relationship? How are these goals being scheduled?

- **Goals**
-
-
-
-

- **Struggles**
-
-
-
-

- **Successes**
-
-
-
-

Talk to God about your goals and struggles. Rejoice and thank God for your growth and successes!

~Evening 1~

~ Write in your calendar how you fellowshipped with God in:

R.A.Y.S.:

* **R**esting in His presence, **"casting all your anxiety on Him, because He cares for you" (1 Peter 5:7, NASB)**,

* **A**ppreciation of Him, even amidst hardship,

* **Y**oke with Christ of love toward others, and

* **S**itting at His feet to listen to His teaching.

(Sample **R.A.Y.S.** reflection, using check marks to describe victories and x marks to describe struggles)

Green, Yellow, and Red Weeks

During your weekly* "Prayer Platoon Discussions" you will be asked if you had a "Green, Yellow, or Red Week."

A "Green Week" means that you had overall victory in **R.A.Y.S**. You do not need to go into detail with the others.

A "Yellow Week" means that you struggled in **R.A.Y.S.** a few times during the week. Discuss the details of your struggles from the notes in your calendar.

A "Red Week" means that you struggled massively in **R.A.Y.S.** during the week. Discuss the details of your struggles from the notes in your calendar.

If your Prayer Platoon is remote, you can agree to email one another weekly and explain what "color" of week you had with details (if needed).

~ Pray for your evening and tomorrow's schedule

~Morning 2~
The Fellowship of Loving Others

Lord, help us defend our prayer lives, for our fellowship with You is hindered by...

1. Preferring traditions rather than mercy
   a. **"But you [Pharisees] say it is all right for people to say to their parents, 'Sorry, I can't help you. For I have vowed to give to God what I would have given to you.' In this way you let them disregard their needy parents. And so you cancel the word of God in order to hand down your own traditions. And this is only one example among many others" (Mark 7:11-13, NLT).**
2. Not caring for the poor
   a. **"Whoever shuts their ears to the cry of the poor will also cry out and not be answered" (Proverbs 21:13, NIV).**

How do these verses describe fellowship with darkness or fellowship with God?

_____

_____

_____

_____

_____

_____

_____

_____

Talk to God about your struggles in these areas.

_____

_____

_____

_____

_____

_____

Seek strength from God to fellowship with Him. **"If anyone serves, they should do so with the strength God provides, so that in all things God may be praised through Jesus Christ. To him be the glory and the power for ever and ever. Amen"** (1 Peter 4:11b, NIV).

_____

_____

_____

_____

_____

_____

Jesus, we draw near to You. You said,

"I am the light of the world. He who follows Me shall not walk in darkness, but have the light of life" (John 8:12, NKJV).

1) Daily prayers & prayer for today's schedule

2) Believers *(Names beginning with the letter 'B')*

-
-
-
-
-
-
-
-
-

3) Unbelievers & People Groups

-
-
-
-
-
-
-

Every other day of this devotional we focus on the last reached people groups. The "last of the last" people groups to be reached are called "level zero" groups. This means they have no Bible translation in progress nor do they have anyone working to reach them. According to www.peoplegroups.org, there are about 586 of these "last of the last" to be reached. These are listed below.

Pray for (1) receptive hearts, (2) missionaries to be sent, and (3) Bible translations to be started. From slavery in Egypt **(Exodus 3:9)** to the first days of the church **(Acts 1:14)** to modern revivals, it is clear that redemptive movements of God are preceded by vigilant prayer movements of His people. Though God's workers may be the tip of an arrow that goes to dark places, your prayers are the bowstring and God is the Archer.

Though the following statistics were taken from www.peoplegroups.org recently, visit the website to see the progress of reaching these groups and other people groups.

www.peoplegroups.org has brilliantly arranged these people groups by country, people group name, and population. A more detailed description of each people group (including maps of their locations and ethnographical research data) can be found at www.ethnologue.com .

Level Zero Groups: Afghanistan - Brazil

"When [Jesus] saw the crowds, he had compassion for them, because they were harassed and helpless, like sheep without a shepherd. Then he said to his disciples, 'The harvest is plentiful, but the laborers are few; therefore pray earnestly to the Lord of the harvest to send out laborers into his harvest'" (Matthew 9:36-38, ESV).

CountryName	PeopleGroup	Population
Afghanistan	Deaf Afghans	119000
Afghanistan	Judeo-Persian Jews	11842
Afghanistan	Moghol	6608
Afghanistan	Pahlavani	3378
Afghanistan	Parya	2056
Albania	Deaf Albanians	16743
Algeria	Berber, Gourara	44627
Algeria	Berber, Tidikelt	16160
Algeria	Berber, Tuat	68680
Algeria	Chenoua	81810
Algeria	Deaf Algerians	222000
Angola	Deaf Angolans	63400
Argentina	Deaf Argentines	228396
Argentina	Tehuelche	200
Armenia	Deaf Armenians	16200
Azerbaijan	Budukh	6146
Azerbaijan	Deaf Azerbaijanis	31000
Azerbaijan	Khinalug	2162
Azerbaijan	Kryz	8877

Azerbaijan	Yergyuch	1138
Bahrain	Deaf Bahrainis	3754
Bangladesh	Koda	1616
Barbados	Deaf Barbadians	1257
Belize	Deaf Belizeans	1531
Benin	Bulba	1828
Benin	Deaf Beninese	34407
Bhutan	Deaf Bhutanese	12044
Bosnia & Herzegovina	Deaf Bosnians	17124
Botswana	Deaf Motswana	8142
Brazil	Akurio	10
Brazil	Amondawa	100
Brazil	Arapaso	537
Brazil	Arutani	17
Brazil	Ava-Canoeiro	17
Brazil	Aweti	171
Brazil	Catawishi	10
Brazil	EnawenÃª-NawÃª	527
Brazil	Guato	700
Brazil	Himarima	80
Brazil	Iapama	200
Brazil	Itogapuk	100
Brazil	Kabixi	100
Brazil	Kashuyana	500
Brazil	Katukina-JutaÃ	600

~Evening 2~

~ Write in your calendar how you fellowshipped with God in:

R.A.Y.S.:

* **R**esting in His presence, **"casting all your anxiety on Him, because He cares for you" (1 Peter 5:7, NASB)**,

* **A**ppreciation of Him, even amidst hardship,

* **Y**oke with Christ of love toward others, and

* **S**itting at His feet to listen to His teaching.

~ Pray for your evening and tomorrow's schedule

*   *   *

~Morning 3~
The Fellowship of Loving Others

Lord, help us defend our prayer lives, for our fellowship with You is hindered by...

3. Bitterness, ungodly anger and ungodly speech
    a. **"But I tell you that anyone who is angry with a brother or sister will be subject to judgment. If you call someone an idiot, you are in danger of being brought before the court. And if you curse someone, you are in danger of the fires of hell" (Matthew 5:22, NIV & NLT).**
4. Refusing to seek reconciliation
    a. **"So if you are presenting a sacrifice at the altar in the Temple and you suddenly remember that someone has something against you, leave your sacrifice there at the altar. Go and be reconciled to that person. Then come and offer your sacrifice to God" (Matthew 5:23, NLT).**

How do these verses describe fellowship with darkness or fellowship with God?

_____

_____

_____

_____

_____
_____
_____
_____

Talk to God about your struggles in these areas.

_____
_____
_____
_____
_____
_____

Seek strength from God to fellowship with Him. **"If anyone serves, they should do so with the strength God provides, so that in all things God may be praised through Jesus Christ. To him be the glory and the power for ever and ever. Amen" (1 Peter 4:11b, NIV).**

_____
_____
_____
_____
_____
_____

Jesus, we draw near to You. You said,

"Yes, I am the gate. Those who come in through me will be saved. They will come and go freely and will find good pastures" (John 10:9, NLT).

1) Daily prayers & prayer for today's schedule

2) Believers *(Names beginning with the letter 'C')*

-
-
-
-
-
-
-
-

3) Unbelievers & People Groups

-
-
-
-
-
-
-
-

Relational Vision & Strategy 2 ~ Children

What are your goals, struggles, and successes in these relationships? How are these goals being scheduled?

- Goals
-
-
-
-
- Struggles
-
-
-
-
- Successes
-
-
-
-

Talk to God about your goals and struggles. Rejoice and thank God for your growth and successes!

~Evening 3~

~ Write in your calendar how you fellowshipped with God in:

R.A.Y.S.:

* **R**esting in His presence, **"casting all your anxiety on Him, because He cares for you" (1 Peter 5:7, NASB)**,

* **A**ppreciation of Him, even amidst hardship,

* **Y**oke with Christ of love toward others, and

* **S**itting at His feet to listen to His teaching.

~ Pray for your evening and tomorrow's schedule

*   *   *

~Morning 4~
The Fellowship of Loving Others

Lord, help us defend our prayer lives, for our fellowship with You is hindered by...

5. Overextending oneself and breaking one's word
   a. **"Just say a simple, 'Yes, I will,' or 'No, I won't.' Anything beyond this is from the evil one" (Matthew 5:37, NLT).**
6. Lying
   a. **"...Pay attention to my prayer, for it comes from honest lips" (Psalm 17:1b, NLT).**

How do these verses describe fellowship with darkness or fellowship with God?

_____

_____

_____

_____

_____

_____

_____

_____

Talk to God about your struggles in these areas.

_____

_____

_____

_____

_____

_____

Seek strength from God to fellowship with Him. **"If anyone serves, they should do so with the strength God provides, so that in all things God may be praised through Jesus Christ. To him be the glory and the power for ever and ever. Amen" (1 Peter 4:11b, NIV).**

_____

_____

_____

_____

_____

_____

Jesus, we draw near to You. You said,

"I am the good shepherd. The good shepherd sacrifices his life for the sheep" (John 10:11, NLT).

1) Daily prayers & prayer for today's schedule

2) Believers *(Names beginning with the letter 'D')*

-
-
-
-
-
-
-
-

3) Unbelievers & People Groups

-
-
-
-
-
-
-
-
-

Level Zero Groups: Brazil – Burkina Faso

"But you will receive power when the Holy Spirit comes upon you. And you will be my witnesses, telling people about me everywhere--in Jerusalem, throughout Judea, in Samaria, and to the ends of the earth" (Acts 1:8, NLT).

Brazil	Korubo	500
Brazil	Kreye	30
Brazil	Mandawaka	24
Brazil	Matipuhy-Nahukua	119
Brazil	Miriti-Tapuia	120
Brazil	Morerebi	100
Brazil	Pokanga	165
Brazil	Sabanes	180
Brazil	Sakirabia	103
Brazil	Saluma	300
Brazil	Sikiana	33
Brazil	Tapirape	601
Brazil	Trumai	198
Brazil	Txikao	402
Brazil	Uncontacted of Bararati	21
Brazil	" " of Cumina	21
Brazil	" " of Curuca	20
Brazil	Uncontacted of IgarapÃ© Tabocal	21
Brazil	Uncontacted of Jandiatuba	300
Brazil	Uncontacted of Madeirinha	21

Brazil	Uncontacted of Mapuera	21
Brazil	Uncontacted of Parauari	21
Brazil	Uncontacted of Quixito	200
Brazil	Uncontacted of Rio Candeias	21
Brazil	Uncontacted of Rio Liberdade	21
Brazil	Uncontacted of Rio Tapirapé	21
Brazil	Uncontacted of Sao Jose	300
Brazil	Uncontacted of Serra do Taquaral	50
Brazil	Uncontacted of Teles Pires	21
Brazil	Uraparaquara	100
Brazil	Uru-Pa-In	200
Brazil	Wayoro	77
Brazil	Wokarangma	31
Brazil	Xeta	86
Brazil	Zoe	421
Brunei	Deaf Bruneians	2003
Brunei	Tutung	9000
Bulgaria	Deaf Bulgarians	37185
Burkina Faso	Deaf Burkinabes	55293

~Evening 4~

~ Write in your calendar how you fellowshipped with God in:

R.A.Y.S.:

* **R**esting in His presence, **"casting all your anxiety on Him, because He cares for you" (1 Peter 5:7, NASB)**,

* **A**ppreciation of Him, even amidst hardship,

* **Y**oke with Christ of love toward others, and

* **S**itting at His feet to listen to His teaching.

~ Pray for your evening and tomorrow's schedule

*   *   *

~Morning 5~
The Fellowship of Loving Others

Lord, help us defend our prayer lives, for our fellowship with You is hindered by...

7. Condemnation, judging, and unforgiveness
   a. "Be merciful, just as your Father is merciful. Do not judge, and you will not be judged. Do not condemn, and you will not be condemned. Forgive and you will be forgiven" (Luke 6:36, 37, NIV).
8. A spirit of vengeance
   a. "You have heard the law that says the punishment must match the injury: 'An eye for an eye, and a tooth for a tooth.' But I say, do not resist an evil person! If someone slaps you on the right cheek, offer the other cheek also" (Matthew 5:39, 40, NLT).
9. Hatred
   a. "If your enemy is hungry, give him some food to eat, and if he is thirsty, give him some water to drink. [In this way] you will make him feel guilty and ashamed, and the LORD will reward you" (Proverbs 25:21, 22, GWT).
   b. "Whoever claims to love God yet hates a brother or sister is a liar" (1 John 4:20a, NIV).

How do these verses describe fellowship with darkness or fellowship with God?

_____
_____
_____
_____
_____
_____
_____
_____

Talk to God about your struggles in these areas.

_____
_____
_____
_____
_____
_____

Seek strength from God to fellowship with Him. **"If anyone serves, they should do so with the strength God provides, so that in all things God may be praised through Jesus Christ. To him be the glory and the power for ever and ever. Amen" (1 Peter 4:11b, NIV).**

_____
_____
_____
_____
_____
_____

Jesus, we draw near to You. You said,

"I am the resurrection and the life. Anyone who believes in me will live, even after dying. Everyone who lives in me and believes in me will never ever die" (John 11:25, NLT).

1) Daily prayers & prayer for today's schedule

2) Believers *(Names beginning with the letter 'E')*

-
-
-
-
-
-
-
-

3) Unbelievers & People Groups

-
-
-
-
-
-

Relational Vision & Strategy 3 ~ Parents

What are your goals, struggles, and successes in these relationships? How are these goals being scheduled?

- **Goals**
-
-
-
-
- **Struggles**
-
-
-
-
- **Successes**
-
-
-
-

Talk to God about your goals and struggles. Rejoice and thank God for your growth and successes!

~Evening 5~

~ Write in your calendar how you fellowshipped with God in:

R.A.Y.S.:

* **R**esting in His presence, **"casting all your anxiety on Him, because He cares for you" (1 Peter 5:7, NASB),**

* **A**ppreciation of Him, even amidst hardship,

* **Y**oke with Christ of love toward others, and

* **S**itting at His feet to listen to His teaching.

~ Pray for your evening and tomorrow's schedule

*　　　　*　　　　*

~Morning 6~
The Fellowship of Loving Others

Lord, help us defend our prayer lives, for our fellowship with You is hindered by...

10. Undercommunicating God's ways to others
    a. **"Without prophetic vision people run wild, but blessed are those who follow [God's] teachings" (Proverbs 29:18, GWT).**
11. Neglecting to oversee and pastor others
    a. **"Be shepherds of God's flock that is under your care, watching over them—not because you must, but because you are willing, as God wants you to be; not pursuing dishonest gain, but eager to serve" (1 Peter 5:2, NIV).**

How do these verses describe fellowship with darkness or fellowship with God?

_____
_____
_____
_____
_____
_____
_____
_____

Talk to God about your struggles in these areas.

_____
_____
_____
_____
_____
_____

Seek strength from God to fellowship with Him. **"If anyone serves, they should do so with the strength God provides, so that in all things God may be praised through Jesus Christ. To him be the glory and the power for ever and ever. Amen" (1 Peter 4:11b, NIV).**

_____
_____
_____
_____
_____
_____

Father, we come to You through Jesus. He said,

"I am the way, the truth, and the life. No one can come to the Father except through me" (John 14:6, NLT).

1) Daily prayers & prayer for today's schedule

2) Believers *(Names beginning with the letter 'F')*

-
-
-
-
-
-
-
-

3) Unbelievers & People Groups

-
-
-
-
-
-
-
-

Level Zero Groups: Burundi – Chad

"For 'Everyone who calls on the name of the LORD will be saved.' But how can they call on him to save them unless they believe in him? And how can they believe in him if they have never heard about him? And how can they hear about him unless someone tells them? And how will anyone go and tell them without being sent? That is why the Scriptures say, 'How beautiful are the feet of messengers who bring good news!'" (Romans 10:13-15, NLT).

Burundi	Deaf Burundians	37190
Cambodia	Deaf Cambodians	73565
Cameroon	Baldamu	234
Cameroon	Beezen	637
Cameroon	Bomwali	6452
Cameroon	Deaf Cameroonians	70567
Cameroon	Dimbong	149
Cameroon	Dumbule	106
Cameroon	Hijuk	606
Cameroon	Jina	4921
Cameroon	Majera	3281
Cameroon	Ndemli	7546
Cameroon	Pam	76
Canada	Brunei	4761
Canada	Grenadian	9846
Canada	Kutenai	321
Canada	Pentlatch	52

Canada	Saint Vincentian	10721
Canada	West Indian Blacks	7526
Cape Verde	Deaf Cape Verdeans	2308
Central African Republic	Benkonjo	2746
Central African Republic	Deaf Central Africans	19075
Central African Republic	Geme	755
Chad	Amdang	63675
Chad	Baxa	1711
Chad	Berguid	11037
Chad	Bernde	7087
Chad	Bolgo Durag	2283
Chad	Bon Gula	1522
Chad	Boor	249
Chad	Buso	62
Chad	Dama	2630
Chad	Deaf Chadians	51939
Chad	Fanya	1395

~Evening 6~

~ Write in your calendar how you fellowshipped with God in:

R.A.Y.S.:

* **R**esting in His presence, **"casting all your anxiety on Him, because He cares for you" (1 Peter 5:7, NASB)**,

* **A**ppreciation of Him, even amidst hardship,

* **Y**oke with Christ of love toward others, and

* **S**itting at His feet to listen to His teaching.

~ Pray for your evening and tomorrow's schedule

*   *   *

~Morning 7~
The Fellowship of Loving Others

Lord, help us defend our prayer lives, for our fellowship with You is hindered by...

12. A lack of planning to maintain our relationships (Planning ahead helps to avoid chaos. Chaos destroys relationships.)
    a. **"a sensible person watches his step" (Proverbs 14:15b, GWT).**
13. Planning our course without seeking God's will
    a. **"I know, LORD, that our lives are not our own. We are not able to plan our own course" (Jeremiah 10:23, NLT).**
14. Neglecting all kinds of relationships and not seeking wholeness in them
    a. **"Blessed are the peacemakers, for they will be called children of God" (Matthew 5:9, NIV).**

How do these verses describe fellowship with darkness or fellowship with God?

_____

_____

_____

_____

_____

_____

_____

_____

Talk to God about your struggles in these areas.

_____

_____

_____

_____

_____

_____

Seek strength from God to fellowship with Him. **"If anyone serves, they should do so with the strength God provides, so that in all things God may be praised through Jesus Christ. To him be the glory and the power for ever and ever. Amen" (1 Peter 4:11b, NIV).**

_____

_____

_____

_____

_____

_____

Jesus, we draw near to You. You said,

"Yes, I am the vine; you are the branches. Those who remain in me, and I in them, will produce much fruit. For apart from me you can do nothing" (John 15:5, NLT).

1) Daily prayers & prayer for today's schedule

2) Believers *(Names beginning with the letter 'G')*

-
-
-
-
-
-
-
-

3) Unbelievers & People Groups

-
-
-
-
-
-
-

Relational Vision & Strategy 4 ~ Distressed Neighbors/Poor

What are your goals, struggles, and successes in these relationships? How are these goals being scheduled?

- Goals
-
-
-
-
- Struggles
-
-
-
- Successes
-
-
-
-

Talk to God about your goals and struggles. Rejoice and thank God for your growth and successes!

~Evening 7~

~ Write in your calendar how you fellowshipped with God in:

R.A.Y.S.:

* **R**esting in His presence, **"casting all your anxiety on Him, because He cares for you" (1 Peter 5:7, NASB)**,

* **A**ppreciation of Him, even amidst hardship,

* **Y**oke with Christ of love toward others, and

* **S**itting at His feet to listen to His teaching.

~ Pray for your evening and tomorrow's schedule

*   *   *

PRAYER PLATOON DISCUSSION 2:

Part I. Review the War Plan for Loving Others

To be in right relationship with others is to put on **"love as a breastplate" (Ephesians 6: 14, NIV)** in your war to abide in Christ.

1) Which verses from the past week have helped you in your prayer life? Which verses challenge you?

_____
_____
_____

2) Regarding fellowshipping with God in **R.A.Y.S.**, did you have a Green, Yellow, or Red week?

_____
_____
_____

3) What are some personal activities you can do to lovingly serve others?

_____

_____

_____

The following are some suggestions for improving your relationships with others:

i. **Make plans to bless your spouse and children. Communicate regularly about these plans with them. Perhaps you can have a weekly coffee date to talk.**

ii. **Communicate with your parents regularly, which is one way to care for them.**

iii. **Prayerfully seek one way to bless the poor (only one because you can't do everything).**

iv. **Consider how to better manage your time. Find a couple of ways to improve your time management, such as keeping a journal or calendar or wearing a watch.**

v. **Before meeting with others, ask God for at least a flicker of love for them. Prepare yourself to say and do all things in a spirit of love.**

It is a blessing to bring more and more order and peace into our lives. It is written, **"The wisdom of the prudent is to give thought to their ways…" (Proverbs 14:8a, NIV)**. It is also written, **"If I give away all I have, and if I deliver up my body to be burned, but have not love, I gain nothing" (1 Corinthians 13:3, ESV)**. Protect your relationship with Christ through serving others in love and with order.

Part II. Introduction to Prayer Battleground Two: *The Fellowship of Listening to Christ*

4. Do you see Bible Study primarily as a duty or primarily as listening to the One you love?

_____

_____

_____

Memory Verse
"...Mary sat at the Lord's feet and listened to his teaching" (Luke 10:39, ESV).

Introduction: The Warfare Against Listening to our Beloved Savior and King

5. How has your study of God's Word led you to repentance recently?

_____

_____

_____

Christ taught, **"I am the true grapevine, and my Father is the gardener. He cuts off every branch of mine that doesn't produce fruit, and he prunes the branches that do bear fruit so they will produce even more" (John 15:1, 2, NLT)**. Thus, repentance (the image of pruning) leads us to bearing more fruit among the nations. The Holy Spirit leads us in repentance as He was sent to, **"...convict the world of its sin..." (John 16:8b, NLT)**. In addition, the Spirit reminds us of Christ's words. It is written, **"But the Helper, the Holy Spirit, whom the Father will send in my name, he will teach you all things and bring to your remembrance all that I have said to you" (John 14:26, ESV)**.

6. What obstacles do you face in spending time in God's Word?

_____

_____

_____

    Satan, in order to block your way from abiding in Christ, desires to keep you in bondage to <u>ignorance and the disobeying of the Word of Christ</u>, that you might not bear fruit. Some of the following verses illustrate bondage to <u>forms of ignorance and the disobeying of Christ's Words</u>, which hinder our prayers. Others of the following verses demonstrate how to abide in Christ through vigilantly listening to Him. Take time to reflect on these verses daily so that you can defend your prayer life. See "Day 29" for a sample Bible Study method.

*   *   *

~Morning 8~
The Fellowship of Listening to Christ

Lord, help us defend our prayer lives, for our fellowship with You is hindered by...

1) Being busy rather than listening to Christ
   - "But the Lord said to [the sister of Mary], 'My dear Martha, you are worried and upset over all these details!" (Luke 10:41, NLT).
2) Cherishing sin
   - "If I had cherished sin in my heart, the Lord would not have listened" (Psalm 66:18, NIV).
3) Not running from sin
   - "Now flee from youthful lusts and pursue righteousness, faith, love and peace, with those who call on the Lord from a pure heart" (2 Timothy 2:22, NASB).
   - "Run from sexual sin!" (1 Corinthians 6:18a, NLT).
   - "She [Potiphar's wife] came and grabbed him [Joseph] by his cloak, demanding, 'Come on, sleep with me!' Joseph tore himself away, but he left his cloak in her hand as he ran from the house" (Genesis 39:12, NLT).

*How do these verses describe fellowship with darkness
or fellowship with God?*

_____

_____

_____

_____

_____

_____

_____

Talk to God about your struggles in these areas.

_____

_____

_____

_____

_____

_____

Seek strength from God to fellowship with Him. **"If
anyone serves, they should do so with the strength
God provides, so that in all things God may be praised
through Jesus Christ. To him be the glory and the
power for ever and ever. Amen" (1 Peter 4:11b, NIV).**

_____

_____

_____

_____

_____

Jesus, we draw near to You. You said,

"I am the bread of life. Whoever comes to me will never be hungry again. Whoever believes in me will never be thirsty" (John 6:35, NLT).

1) Daily prayers & prayer for today's schedule

2) Believers *(Names beginning with the letter 'H')*

-
-
-
-
-
-
-
-

3) Unbelievers & People Groups

-
-
-
-
-
-
-
-

Level Zero Groups: Chad – China

"Go therefore and make disciples of all nations, baptizing them in the name of the Father and of the Son and of the Holy Spirit, teaching them to observe all that I have commanded you. And behold, I am with you always, to the end of the age" (Matthew 28:19, 20, ESV).

Chad	Fongoro	1384
Chad	Goundo	33
Chad	Gula	13063
Chad	Jaya	3205
Chad	Jegu	1865
Chad	Kajakse	14002
Chad	Karanga	12434
Chad	Kendeje	1426
Chad	Koke	892
Chad	Kujarge	1384
Chad	Majera	2749
Chad	Marfa	185349
Chad	Maslam	837
Chad	Mawa	8098
Chad	Mesmedje	32328
Chad	Mimi	11783
Chad	Mogum	8704
Chad	Mubi	43891
Chad	Surbakhal	6921
Chad	Tana	30805
Chad	Torom	10729
Chad	Ubi	1368

Chad	Vale	773
Chile	Deaf Chileans	62946
China	Ai-Cham	3340
China	Ainu	8281
China	Angku	8038
China	A'ou	2345
China	Baima	17443
China	Bit	760
China	Bonan	12056
China	Bugan	3813
China	Buyang	3634
China	De'ang, Shwe	6901
China	Dianbao	11586
China	E	36548
China	Enipu	20868
China	Ga Mong	56950
China	Gepo, Western	8300
China	Guaigun	522
China	Hagei	2663
China	Hu	1662
China	Kemei	1435
China	Kong Ge	1573
China	Lalu, Xuzhang	5217
China	Lalu, Yangliu	48225
China	Lati	2462
China	Linghua	25005
China	Lolo, Southeastern	45808
China	Luzu	1248

~Evening 8~

~ Write in your calendar how you fellowshipped with God in:

R.A.Y.S.:

* **R**esting in His presence, **"casting all your anxiety on Him, because He cares for you" (1 Peter 5:7, NASB)**,

* **A**ppreciation of Him, even amidst hardship,

* **Y**oke with Christ of love toward others, and

* **S**itting at His feet to listen to His teaching.

~ Pray for your evening and tomorrow's schedule

*   *   *

~Morning 9~
The Fellowship of Listening to Christ

Lord, help us defend our prayer lives, for our fellowship with You is hindered by...

4) Disobeying God's commandments
   - **"[We] receive from Him anything we ask, because we keep his commands and do what pleases Him" (1 John 3:22, NIV).**

5) Self-righteousness
   - [First, a self-righteous person prayed at the Temple,] **"But the tax collector stood at a distance. He would not even look up to heaven, but beat his breast and said, 'God have mercy on me, a sinner.' I tell you that this man, rather than the other [self-righteous person], went home justified before God. For all those who exalt themselves will be humbled, and those who humble themselves will be exalted" (Luke 18:13, 14, NIV).**

How do these verses describe fellowship with darkness or fellowship with God?

_____

_____

_____

_____

_____

_____

_____

_____

Talk to God about your struggles in these areas.

_____

_____

_____

_____

_____

_____

Seek strength from God to fellowship with Him. **"If anyone serves, they should do so with the strength God provides, so that in all things God may be praised through Jesus Christ. To him be the glory and the power for ever and ever. Amen" (1 Peter 4:11b, NIV).**

_____

_____

_____

_____

_____

_____

Jesus, we draw near to You. You said,

"I am the light of the world. He who follows Me shall not walk in darkness, but have the light of life" (John 8:12, NKJV).

1) Daily prayers & prayer for today's schedule

2) Believers *(Names beginning with the letter 'I')*

-
-
-
-
-
-
-
-
-

3) Unbelievers & People Groups

-
-
-
-
-
-
-

Relational Vision & Strategy 5 ~ Hospitality to Outsiders

What are your goals, struggles, and successes in these relationships? How are these goals being scheduled?

- **Goals**
-
-
-

- **Struggles**
-
-
-

- **Successes**
-
-
-

Talk to God about your goals and struggles. Rejoice and thank God for your growth and successes!

~Evening 9~

~ Write in your calendar how you fellowshipped with God in:

R.A.Y.S.:

* **R**esting in His presence, **"casting all your anxiety on Him, because He cares for you" (1 Peter 5:7, NASB)**,

* **A**ppreciation of Him, even amidst hardship,

* **Y**oke with Christ of love toward others, and

* **S**itting at His feet to listen to His teaching.

~ Pray for your evening and tomorrow's schedule

*   *   *

~Morning 10~
The Fellowship of Listening to Christ

Lord, help us defend our prayer lives, for our fellowship with You is hindered by...

6) Wrong motives.
   - **"When you ask, you do not receive, because you ask with wrong motives, that you may spend what you get on your pleasures" (James 4:3, NIV).**

7) Ignorance of God's will
   - **"This is the confidence we have in approaching God: That if we ask anything according to His will, he hears us" (1 John 5:14, NIV).**

How do these verses describe fellowship with darkness or fellowship with God?

_____

_____

_____

_____

_____

_____

_____

_____

Talk to God about your struggles in these areas.

_____

_____

_____

_____

_____

_____

Seek strength from God to fellowship with Him. **"If anyone serves, they should do so with the strength God provides, so that in all things God may be praised through Jesus Christ. To him be the glory and the power for ever and ever. Amen" (1 Peter 4:11b, NIV).**

_____

_____

_____

_____

_____

_____

Jesus, we draw near to You. You said,

"Yes, I am the gate. Those who come in through me will be saved. They will come and go freely and will find good pastures" (John 10:9, NLT).

1) Daily prayers & prayer for today's schedule

2) Believers *(Names beginning with the letter 'J')*

-
-
-
-
-
-
-
-
-

3) Unbelievers & People Groups

-
-
-
-
-
-
-

Level Zero Groups: China – Congo, DRC

"You then, my child, be strengthened by the grace that is in Christ Jesus, and what you have heard from me in the presence of many witnesses entrust to faithful men who will be able to teach others also" (2 Timothy 2:1, 2, ESV).

China	Manyak	2332
China	Menia	1412
China	Micha	1188
China	Mili	29903
China	Monba, Cona	41326
China	Mozhihei	5297
China	Pengzi	297
China	Popei	5959
China	Suan	297
China	Tajik, Sarikoli	41404
China	Teleut	65
China	Tuerke	215
China	Wunai	11573
China	Xi	1428
China	Yerong	620
China	Yongchun	14715
Colombia	Cabiyari	277
Colombia	Carabayo	300
Colombia	Eastern Tunebo	300
Colombia	Embera-Baudo	5000
Colombia	Macaguan	542
Colombia	Playero	150

Colombia	Tunebo, Angosturas	50
Colombia	Yari	700
Comoros	Deaf Comorans	3524
Congo	Deaf Congolese	17243
Congo	Mbangwe	2111
Congo	Minduumo	4637
Congo	Ngondi	3750
Congo, DRC	Deaf Congolese	343179
Congo, DRC	Koguru	6740
Congo, DRC	Lonzo	453
Congo, DRC	Ndobo	14032
Congo, DRC	Ndunga	5415
Congo, DRC	Ngbinda	7636
Congo, DRC	Ngundu	7636
Congo, DRC	Pelende	10869
Congo, DRC	Samba	5434
Congo, DRC	Seba	241493
Congo, DRC	Sere	9399
Congo, DRC	Songora	4993
Congo, DRC	Tagbo	30839
Congo, DRC	Yakoma	14685
Congo, DRC	Yamongeri	22762

~Evening 10~

~ Write in your calendar how you fellowshipped with God in:

R.A.Y.S.:

* **R**esting in His presence, **"casting all your anxiety on Him, because He cares for you" (1 Peter 5:7, NASB)**,

* **A**ppreciation of Him, even amidst hardship,

* **Y**oke with Christ of love toward others, and

* **S**itting at His feet to listen to His teaching.

~ Pray for your evening and tomorrow's schedule

*   *   *

~Morning 11~
The Fellowship of Listening to Christ

Lord, help us defend our prayer lives, for our fellowship with You is hindered by...

8) Misrepresenting God
   - **"My servant Job will pray for you, and I will accept his prayer on your behalf. I will not treat you as you deserve, for you have not spoken accurately about me, as my servant Job has" (Job 42:8b, NLT).**

9) Not sharing the Scriptures
   - **"The Spirit of the Lord speaks through me; his Words are upon my tongue" (2 Samuel 23:2, NLT).**

10) Not giving nor receiving godly counsel
    - **"Timely advice is lovely, like golden apples in a silver basket" (Proverbs 25:11, NLT).**
    - **"Plans fail for lack of counsel, but with many advisers they succeed" (Proverbs 14:22, NIV).**

How do these verses describe fellowship with darkness or fellowship with God?

_____

_____

_____

_____

_____

_____

_____

_____

Talk to God about your struggles in these areas.

_____

_____

_____

_____

_____

Seek strength from God to fellowship with Him. **"If anyone serves, they should do so with the strength God provides, so that in all things God may be praised through Jesus Christ. To him be the glory and the power for ever and ever. Amen" (1 Peter 4:11b, NIV).**

_____

_____

_____

_____

_____

Jesus, we draw near to You. You said,

"I am the good shepherd. The good shepherd sacrifices his life for the sheep" (John 10:11, NLT).

1) Daily prayers & prayer for today's schedule

2) Believers *(Names beginning with the letter 'K')*

-
-
-
-
-
-
-
-
-

3) Unbelievers & People Groups

-
-
-
-
-
-
-
-

Relational Vision & Strategy 6 ~ Temple Maintenance

It is written, **"Dear friend, I hope all is well with you and that you are as healthy in body as you are strong in spirit" (3 John 2, NLT)**. What are your goals, struggles, and successes for your own health? How are these goals being scheduled?

- Goals
-
-
-
-
- Struggles
-
-
-
-
- Successes
-
-
-
-

Talk to God about your goals and struggles. Rejoice and thank God for your growth and successes!

~Evening 11~

~ Write in your calendar how you fellowshipped with God in:

R.A.Y.S.:

* **R**esting in His presence, **"casting all your anxiety on Him, because He cares for you" (1 Peter 5:7, NASB)**,

* **A**ppreciation of Him, even amidst hardship,

* **Y**oke with Christ of love toward others, and

* **S**itting at His feet to listen to His teaching.

~ Pray for your evening and tomorrow's schedule

*　　　　*　　　　*

~Morning 12~
The Fellowship of Listening to Christ

Lord, help us defend our prayer lives, for our fellowship with You is hindered by...

11) Not testing other's counsel against the Word of God

- **"...do not despise prophetic utterances, But examine everything carefully; hold fast to that which is good" (1 Thessalonians 5:20, 21, NASB).**

12) Not warning others of the wrong path and hell

- **"When I say to a wicked person, 'You will surely die,' and you do not warn them or speak out to dissuade them from their evil ways in order to save their life, that person will die for their sin, and I will hold you accountable for their blood" (Ezekiel 3:18, NIV).**

How do these verses describe fellowship with darkness or fellowship with God?

_____

_____

_____

_____

_____

_____

_____

_____

Talk to God about your struggles in these areas.

_____

_____

_____

_____

_____

_____

Seek strength from God to fellowship with Him. **"If anyone serves, they should do so with the strength God provides, so that in all things God may be praised through Jesus Christ. To him be the glory and the power for ever and ever. Amen" (1 Peter 4:11b, NIV).**

_____

_____

_____

_____

_____

_____

Jesus, we draw near to You. You said,

"I am the resurrection and the life. Anyone who believes in me will live, even after dying. Everyone who lives in me and believes in me will never ever die" (John 11:25, NLT).

1) Daily prayers & prayer for today's schedule

2) Believers *(Names beginning with the letter 'L')*

-
-
-
-
-
-
-
-
-

3) Unbelievers & People Groups

-
-
-
-
-
-

Level Zero Groups: Congo, DRC – Gabon

"Declare his glory among the nations, his marvelous works among all the peoples!" (Psalm 96:3, ESV).

Congo, DRC	Yela	48569
Congo, DRC	Yulu-Binga	734
Cote d'Ivoire	Deaf Ivorians	87151
Cote d'Ivoire	Komono	6468
Cote d'Ivoire	Konyanke	16487
Croatia	Deaf Croatians	17294
Cuba	Deaf Cubans	54237
Cyprus	Deaf Cypriots	3933
Denmark	Danish Travellers	3155
Denmark	Deaf Danish	24400
Djibouti	Deaf Djiboutians	3609
Egypt	Berber, Siwa	12434
Equatorial Guinea	Deaf Equatoguineans	3002
Equatorial Guinea	Yasa	1131
Eritrea	Deaf Eritreans	25519
Eritrea	Nara	97399
Estonia	Deaf Estonians	6292
Ethiopia	Anfillo	1642
Ethiopia	Baiso	1493
Ethiopia	Bale	7001
Ethiopia	Begi-Mao	50224
Ethiopia	Deaf Ethiopians	390042
Ethiopia	Dorze	65515

Ethiopia	Ganza	8058
Ethiopia	Kachama	698
Ethiopia	Karo	1689
Ethiopia	Langa	5834
Ethiopia	Maji	41970
Ethiopia	Melo	119391
Ethiopia	Mesmes	15403
Ethiopia	Nara	61331
Ethiopia	Northern Mao	11339
Ethiopia	Seze	4201
Ethiopia	Shanquilla	31
Ethiopia	Tabi	3452
Ethiopia	Xamir	208775
Ethiopia	Yidinit	700
Fiji	Deaf Fijians	3661
French Guiana	Deaf Guyanese	965
Gabon	Barama	7917

~Evening 12~

~ Write in your calendar how you fellowshipped with God in:

R.A.Y.S.:

* **R**esting in His presence, **"casting all your anxiety on Him, because He cares for you" (1 Peter 5:7, NASB)**,

* **A**ppreciation of Him, even amidst hardship,

* **Y**oke with Christ of love toward others, and

* **S**itting at His feet to listen to His teaching.

~ Pray for your evening and tomorrow's schedule

*   *   *

~Morning 13~
The Fellowship of Listening to Christ

Lord, help us defend our prayer lives, for our fellowship with You is hindered by…

13) Not encouraging others through the speaking & serving gifts
   - **"He makes the whole body fit together perfectly. As each part does its own special work, it helps the other parts grow, so that the whole body is healthy and growing and full of love" (Ephesians 4:16, NLT).**

14) Not restraining one's speech
   - [There is] **"A time to be quiet and a time to speak" (Ecclesiastes 3:7b, NLT).**
   - **"Therefore the prudent keep quiet in such times, for the times are evil" (Amos 5:13, NIV).**
   - **"Don't waste what is holy on people who are unholy. Don't throw your pearls to pigs! They will trample the pearls, then turn and attack you" (Matthew 7:6, NLT).**

How do these verses describe fellowship with darkness or fellowship with God?

_____

_____

_____

_____

_____
_____
_____
_____

Talk to God about your struggles in these areas.

_____
_____
_____
_____
_____
_____

Seek strength from God to fellowship with Him. **"If anyone serves, they should do so with the strength God provides, so that in all things God may be praised through Jesus Christ. To him be the glory and the power for ever and ever. Amen" (1 Peter 4:11b, NIV).**

_____
_____
_____
_____
_____
_____

Father, we come to You through Jesus. He said,

"I am the way, the truth, and the life. No one can come to the Father except through me" (John 14:6, NLT).

1) Daily prayers & prayer for today's schedule

2) Believers *(Names beginning with the letter 'M')*

-
-
-
-
-
-
-
-
-

3) Unbelievers & People Groups

-
-
-
-
-
-
-

Relational Vision & Strategy 7 ~ Leaning on Christ

What are your goals, struggles, and successes in relying on Christ through prayer? How are these goals being scheduled?

Be obsessed with prayer. God desires of us to seek Him regularly and consistently, as it is written, **"Pray without ceasing" (1 Thessalonians 5:17, KJV)**. Unfortunately, there is a widespread misunderstanding that being serious about prayer means that you get up very, very early at 3, 4, or 5 am to pray every single day. For some people, very early morning prayer is their favorite way to meet with Jesus, as it is written, **"I rise before dawn and cry for help" (Psalm 119:147a, NIV)**. For many others who attempt this pattern of prayer, it becomes very legalistic and unrealistic. They soon face their own failure and give up entirely on prayer itself. It is so important that our prayer goals be unique and realistic. God knows the specific and individual challenges in each person's life, such as work schedule, infant sleep patterns, health challenges, etc.

Take time below to list your specific goals for meeting with the Lord (answer the questions: Who, what, when, where, how, and why). Then, consider if the goals are realistic given your unique, God-given situation. Remember that Jesus loves variety. Though He desires for us to be obsessed with prayer, He does not call us all to meet with Him in the exact same ways. Even your own patterns of prayer may change with time.

- Goals
-
-
-
-
-
-
-
- Struggles
-
-
-
-
-
-
- Successes
-
-
-
-
-
-

Talk to God about your goals and struggles.
Rejoice and thank God for your growth and
successes!

~Evening 13~

~ Write in your calendar how you fellowshipped with God in:

R.A.Y.S.:

* **R**esting in His presence, **"casting all your anxiety on Him, because He cares for you" (1 Peter 5:7, NASB)**,

* **A**ppreciation of Him, even amidst hardship,

* **Y**oke with Christ of love toward others, and

* **S**itting at His feet to listen to His teaching.

~ Pray for your evening and tomorrow's schedule

*   *   *

~Morning 14~
The Fellowship of Listening to God

Lord, help us defend our prayer lives, for our fellowship with You is hindered by...

15) Not being moved by God
- **"The Holy Spirit said to Philip, 'Go over and walk along beside the carriage'" (Acts 8:29, NLT).**

16) Not following one's calling
- **"The LORD gave this message to Jonah son of Amittai, 'Get up and go to the great city of Ninevah'" (Jonah 1:1, 2a, NLT).**

How do these verses describe fellowship with darkness or fellowship with God?

_____
_____
_____
_____
_____
_____
_____
_____

Talk to God about your struggles in these areas.

_____

_____

_____

_____

_____

_____

Seek strength from God to fellowship with Him. **"If anyone serves, they should do so with the strength God provides, so that in all things God may be praised through Jesus Christ. To him be the glory and the power for ever and ever. Amen" (1 Peter 4:11b, NIV).**

_____

_____

_____

_____

_____

_____

Jesus, we draw near to You. You said,

"Yes, I am the vine; you are the branches. Those who remain in me, and I in them, will produce much fruit. For apart from me you can do nothing" *(John 15:5, NLT).*

1) Daily prayers & prayer for today's schedule

2) Believers *(Names beginning with the letter 'N')*

-
-
-
-
-
-
-
-
-

3) Unbelievers & People Groups

-
-
-
-
-

"Then I heard the Lord asking, 'Whom should I send as a messenger to this people? Who will go for us?' I said, 'Here I am. Send me'" (Isaiah 6:8, NLT).

Gabon	Deaf Gabonese	6631
Gabon	Minduumo	5466
Gabon	Northern Teke	19911
Gabon	Simba	4731
Georgia	Deaf Georgians	16834
Ghana	Kantosi	2590
Greece	Deaf Greeks	62695
Guinea	Deaf Guineans	27079
Guinea-Bissau	Deaf Guinea-Bissauans	8023
Iceland	Deaf Icelanders	1384
India	Gadaria (Vaghri)	1714
India	Kahar (Shekhawati)	31403
India	Kandera	25425
India	Kudiya	3914
Indonesia	Bonerate	13000
Indonesia	Campalagian	66000
Indonesia	Deaf Indonesians	1057130
Indonesia	Dondo	13000
Indonesia	Geser Gorom	32000
Indonesia	Hitu	16000
Indonesia	Kluet	50000
Indonesia	Makian Barat	40000
Indonesia	Makian Timur	30000

Indonesia	Patani-Maba	6000
Indonesia	Petapa	569
Indonesia	Seit-Kaitetu	12000
Indonesia	Sula	80000
Indonesia	Taluki	569
Indonesia	Tombelala	1252
Indonesia	Topoiyo	2276
Indonesia	Waru	455
Indonesia	Wawonii	27500
Iran	Alviri-Vidari	1000
Iran	Astiani	20300
Iran	Bashkardi	6000
Iran	Deaf Iranians	349643
Iran	Fars	6763
Iran	Gabri	12000
Iran	Gazi	6000
Iran	Gurani Kurd	26000
Iran	Hulaula	300
Iran	Karingani	17580
Iran	Khalaj	40500

~Evening 14~

~ Write in your calendar how you fellowshipped with God in:

R.A.Y.S.:

* **R**esting in His presence, **"casting all your anxiety on Him, because He cares for you" (1 Peter 5:7, NASB)**,

* **A**ppreciation of Him, even amidst hardship,

* **Y**oke with Christ of love toward others, and

* **S**itting at His feet to listen to His teaching.

~ Pray for your evening and tomorrow's schedule

*   *   *

PRAYER PLATOON DISCUSSION 3:

Part I. Review the War Plan for Listening to our Beloved Savior and King

To listen to your Beloved Savior and King and obey Him is to defensively handle **"the sword of the Spirit, which is the word of God" (Ephesians 6:17, NIV)** in your war to abide in Christ.

1) Which verses from the past week have helped you in your prayer life? Which verses challenge you?

_____

_____

_____

2) Regarding fellowshipping with God in **R.A.Y.S.**, did you have a Green, Yellow, or Red week?

_____

_____

_____

3) What are some personal activities you can do to listen more closely to Christ?

_____

_____

_____

The following are some suggestions for listening to the Lord:

i. **Read a passage of Scripture daily (around 10 verses long). Perhaps you can pair this with a cup of coffee. Highlight things you like, such as God's power, His love, and the good path.**

ii. **Re-read the same passage and look for areas about which you need to change your heart and mind. Note places where you need to change your attitudes, beliefs, or actions.**

iii. **Try writing down on an index card a verse you want to memorize. Practice reciting the verse until you can recite it from memory.**

We also model for others listening to our Beloved Savior and King. In doing so, we are a benefit to them, as Paul wrote, **"Whatever you have learned or received or heard from me, or seen in me—put it into practice. And the God of peace will be with you" (Philippians 4:9, NIV)**. Proverbs adds, **"Whoever heeds discipline shows the way of life, but whoever ignores correction leads others astray" (Proverbs 10:17, NIV)**. Protect your relationship with Christ through listening to His voice.

Part II. Introduction to Prayer Battleground Three: *The Fellowship of Praise*

4) On a scale of 1 to 10, with 10 being the highest, how consistently do you keep an attitude of appreciating God even amidst adversity?

_____

_____

_____

Memory Verse
"God is Spirit, and only by the power of his Spirit can people worship him as he really is" (John 4:24, GNT).

Introduction: The Warfare Against Thanksgiving

5) What songs lead you to appreciate and praise God even amidst adversity?

_____

_____

_____

It is written that the Lord, **"inhabits"** the praises of His people (**Psalm 22:3**). The Spirit of God, who resides in

Believers **(John 14:17)**, fellowships with them in glorifying Christ. It is written, **"He [the Holy Spirit] will glorify me, for he will take what is mine and declare it to you" (John 16:14, ESV)**. Jesus glorifies the Father **(Matthew 11:25)** and the Father glorifies the Son **(John 8:54; 17:1, 5)**.

6) What are the obstacles to praising and appreciating God in your life?

_____

_____

_____

       Satan, in order to block your way from abiding in Christ, desires to keep you in bondage to <u>discontentment and complaining</u>, that you might not bear fruit. Some of the following verses illustrate bondage to <u>forms of discontentment or complaining</u>, which hinder your prayers. Others of the following verses demonstrate how to abide in Christ through vigilantly Praising God. Take time to reflect on these verses daily so that you can defend your prayer life.

*   *   *

~Morning 15~
The Fellowship of Praise

Lord, help us defend our prayer lives, for our fellowship with You is hindered by...

1. Complaining (Job modeled for us a path of praising God even in the midst of great loss.)
   - "[and Job] **said, "Naked I came from my mother's womb, and naked I will depart. The LORD gave and the LORD has taken away; may the name of the LORD be praised" (Job 1:21, NIV).**
2. Not enduring amidst persecution (Paul and Silas modeled for us a path of praising God even in the midst of great pain.)
   - [After the two believers were flogged and jailed, it says that,] **"About midnight Paul and Silas were praying and singing hymns to God, and the other prisoners were listening to them" (Acts 16:25, NIV).**

How do these verses describe fellowship with darkness or fellowship with God?

_____

_____

_____

_____

_____

_____

_____

_____

Talk to God about your struggles in these areas.

_____

_____

_____

_____

_____

_____

Seek strength from God to fellowship with Him. **"If anyone serves, they should do so with the strength God provides, so that in all things God may be praised through Jesus Christ. To him be the glory and the power for ever and ever. Amen" (1 Peter 4:11b, NIV).**

_____

_____

_____

_____

_____

_____

Jesus, we draw near to You. You said,

"I am the bread of life. Whoever comes to me will never be hungry again. Whoever believes in me will never be thirsty" (John 6:35, NLT).

1) Daily prayers & prayer for today's schedule

2) Believers *(Names beginning with the letter 'O')*

-
-
-
-
-
-
-
-
-

3) Unbelievers & People Groups

-
-
-
-
-
-
-

Relational Vision & Strategy 8 ~ Leaning on Christ with Others

What are your goals, struggles, and successes in your prayer partner relationships? How are these goals being scheduled?

- Goals
-
-
-
-

- Struggles
-
-
-
-

- Successes
-
-
-
-

Talk to God about your goals and struggles. Rejoice and thank God for your growth and successes!

~Evening 15~

~ Write in your calendar how you fellowshipped with God in:

R.A.Y.S.:

* **R**esting in His presence, **"casting all your anxiety on Him, because He cares for you" (1 Peter 5:7, NASB)**,

* **A**ppreciation of Him, even amidst hardship,

* **Y**oke with Christ of love toward others, and

* **S**itting at His feet to listen to His teaching.

~ Pray for your evening and tomorrow's schedule

*   *   *

~Morning 16~
The Fellowship of Praise

Lord, help us defend our prayer lives, for our fellowship with You is hindered by...

3. Ritualistic worship instead of heartfelt thanksgiving
   - **"Make thankfulness your sacrifice to God and keep the vows you made to the Most High. Then call on Me when you are in trouble and I will rescue you, and you will give me glory" (Psalm 50:14, 15, NLT).**
4. Fear (Daniel modeled for us a path of praising God even in the midst of being threatened.)
   - **"But when Daniel learned that the law [threatening his life] had been signed, he went home and knelt down as usual in his upstairs room, with its windows open toward Jerusalem. He prayed three times a day, just as he had always done, giving thanks to his God" (Daniel 6:10, NLT).**
5. Forgetting God's mercies
   - **"One of them [the ten lepers who were healed], when he saw he was healed, came back, praising God in a loud voice. He threw himself at Jesus' feet and thanked him-and he was a Samaritan. Jesus asked, 'Were not all ten cleansed? Where are the other nine?'" (Luke 17:15-17, NIV).**

How do these verses describe fellowship with darkness or fellowship with God?

_____
_____
_____
_____
_____
_____
_____
_____

Talk to God about your struggles in these areas.

_____
_____
_____
_____
_____
_____

Seek strength from God to fellowship with Him. **"If anyone serves, they should do so with the strength God provides, so that in all things God may be praised through Jesus Christ. To him be the glory and the power for ever and ever. Amen" (1 Peter 4:11b, NIV).**

_____
_____
_____
_____
_____
_____

Jesus, we draw near to You. You said,

"I am the light of the world. He who follows Me shall not walk in darkness, but have the light of life" (John 8:12, NKJV).

1) Daily prayers & prayer for today's schedule

2) Believers *(Names beginning with the letter 'P')*

-
-
-
-
-
-
-
-
-

3) Unbelievers & People Groups

-
-
-
-
-
-
-

Level Zero Groups: Iran – Laos

"Sing to the Lord, all the earth;
proclaim his salvation day after day.
Declare his glory among the nations,
his marvelous deeds among all peoples"
(1 Chronicles 16:23, 24, NIV).

Iran	Khunsari	20300
Iran	Koroshi	1000
Iran	Mussulman Tat	10100
Iran	Natanzi	6700
Iran	Nayini	6700
Iran	Rudbari	500
Iran	Sangisari	16500
Iran	Semnani	30000
Iran	Senaya	57
Iran	Shahmirzadi	6000
Iran	Shahrudi	1000
Iran	Sivandi	6700
Iran	Soi	6700
Iran	Taromi, Upper	1000
Iran	Vafsi	20300
Iraq	Bajelan	34049
Iraq	Deaf Iraqis	189183
Iraq	Hawrami	32308
Iraq	Koi-sanjaq Sooret	1362
Iraq	Luri	114063
Ireland	Deaf Irish	20662
Ireland	Irish Travellers	6030
Israel	Deaf Israelis	38669

Israel	Hula Hula	10243
Italy	Cimbrian	2230
Italy	Deaf Italians	278400
Italy	Dolomite	30000
Italy	Mocheno	1900
Italy	Walser	3400
Jamaica	Deaf Jamaicans	13560
Jordan	Deaf Jordanians	31927
Kazakhstan	Ili Turki	120
Kazakhstan	Bukharic Jews	800
Kuwait	Deaf Kuwaitis	12219
Kyrgyzstan	Bukharic Jews	455
Laos	Bit	1964
Laos	Bo	3816
Laos	Chut	1591
Laos	Deaf Laotians	29161
Laos	Halang Doan	2300

~Evening 16~

~ Write in your calendar how you fellowshipped with God in:

R.A.Y.S.:

* **R**esting in His presence, **"casting all your anxiety on Him, because He cares for you" (1 Peter 5:7, NASB)**,

* **A**ppreciation of Him, even amidst hardship,

* **Y**oke with Christ of love toward others, and

* **S**itting at His feet to listen to His teaching.

~ Pray for your evening and tomorrow's schedule

*   *   *

~Morning 17~
The Fellowship of Praise

Lord, help us defend our prayer lives, for our fellowship with You is hindered by...

6. An unrepentant heart (Jonah modeled for us praising God in the midst of repentance.)

    - [Jonah prayed while in the fish,] **"As my life was slipping away, I remembered the LORD. And my earnest prayer went out to you in your holy temple. Those who worship false gods turn their backs on all God's mercies, But I with the voice of thanksgiving will sacrifice to you; what I have vowed I will pay. Salvation belongs to the LORD!" (Jonah 2:7-9, NLT & ESV).**

7. Choosing sin over revering God (Joseph modeled for us a path of remembering and praising God in the midst of temptation.)

    - **"...'with me in charge,' [Joseph] told [the wife of Potiphar], 'my master does not concern himself with anything in the house, everything he owns he has entrusted to my care. No one is greater in this house than I am. My master has withheld nothing from me except you, because you are his wife. How then could I do such a wicked thing and sin against God?'" (Genesis 39: 8, 9, NIV).**

How do these verses describe fellowship with darkness or fellowship with God?

_____
_____
_____
_____
_____
_____
_____

Talk to God about your struggles in these areas.

_____
_____
_____
_____
_____

Seek strength from God to fellowship with Him. **"If anyone serves, they should do so with the strength God provides, so that in all things God may be praised through Jesus Christ. To him be the glory and the power for ever and ever. Amen" (1 Peter 4:11b, NIV).**

_____
_____
_____
_____
_____

Jesus, we draw near to You. You said,

"Yes, I am the gate. Those who come in through me will be saved. They will come and go freely and will find good pastures" (John 10:9, NLT).

1) Daily prayers & prayer for today's schedule

2) Believers *(Names beginning with the letter 'Q & R')*

-
-
-
-
-
-
-
-
-

3) Unbelievers & People Groups

-
-
-
-
-
-
-

Relational Vision & Strategy 9 ~ Fasting

What are your goals, struggles, and successes in this area? How are these goals being scheduled?

- Goals
-
-
-
-

- Struggles
-
-
-
-

- Successes
-
-
-
-

Talk to God about your goals and struggles. Rejoice and thank God for your growth and successes!

~Evening 17~

~ Write in your calendar how you fellowshipped with God in:

R.A.Y.S.:

* **R**esting in His presence, **"casting all your anxiety on Him, because He cares for you" (1 Peter 5:7, NASB)**,

* **A**ppreciation of Him, even amidst hardship,

* **Y**oke with Christ of love toward others, and

* **S**itting at His feet to listen to His teaching.

~ Pray for your evening and tomorrow's schedule

*   *   *

~Morning 18~
The Fellowship of Praise

Lord, help us defend our prayer lives, for our fellowship with You is hindered by...

8. Preferring worldliness rather than delighting in God's teachings
   - **"Blessed is the person who does not follow the advice of wicked people, take the path of sinners, or join the company of mockers. Rather he delights in the teachings of the LORD and reflects on his teachings day and night" (Psalm 1:1, 2, GWT).**
9. Avoiding God's Word
   - **"Let the Word of Christ dwell in you richly, teaching and admonishing one another in all wisdom, singing Psalms and hymns and spiritual songs, with thankfulness in your hearts to God" (Colossians 3:16, ESV).**

How do these verses describe fellowship with darkness or fellowship with God?

_____

_____

_____

_____

_____

_____

_____

_____

Talk to God about your struggles in these areas.

_____

_____

_____

_____

_____

_____

Seek strength from God to fellowship with Him. **"If anyone serves, they should do so with the strength God provides, so that in all things God may be praised through Jesus Christ. To him be the glory and the power for ever and ever. Amen" (1 Peter 4:11b, NIV).**

_____

_____

_____

_____

_____

_____

Jesus, we draw near to You. You said,

"I am the good shepherd. The good shepherd sacrifices his life for the sheep" (John 10:11, NLT).

1) Daily prayers & prayer for today's schedule

2) Believers *(Names beginning with the letter 'S')*

-
-
-
-
-
-
-
-
-

3) Unbelievers & People Groups

-
-
-
-
-
-
-
-

Level Zero Groups: Laos – Malaysia

"Therefore I will praise you, LORD, among the nations; I will sing the praises of your name" (Psalm 18:49, NIV).

Laos	Hung	4459
Laos	Kate	724
Laos	Khua	3816
Laos	Kuan	3635
Laos	Laoseng	9534
Laos	Mlabri	31
Laos	Nguon	1992
Laos	O'du	317
Laos	Phunoi	51861
Laos	Pong	31124
Laos	Pouhoy	291
Laos	Samtao	3533
Laos	Sila	2574
Laos	Singmoon	6869
Laos	Sou	3053
Laos	Tai He	11642
Laos	Tai Khang	7270
Laos	Tai Laan	582
Laos	Tai Pao	4799
Laos	Tayten	427
Laos	Thae	3777
Laos	Tong	13324
Laos	Yoy	1455
Lebanon	Deaf Lebanese	20955
Lesotho	Deaf Mosotho	9157

Liberia	Deaf Liberians	14207
Libya	Deaf Libyans	35955
Libya	Sawknah	7841
Libya	Wadshili	2914
Libya	Zuara	53465
Lithuania	Deaf Lithuanians	16585
Luxembourg	Deaf Luxembourger	2081
Macedonia	Deaf Macedonians	10385
Madagascar	Deaf Malagasians	87738
Malawi	Deaf Malawians	61755
Malaysia	Deaf Malaysians	135561
Malaysia	Javanese	11487
Malaysia	Kedayan	75000
Malaysia	Kensiu	316
Malaysia	Lahanan	714
Malaysia	Lelak	449

~Evening 18~

~ Write in your calendar how you fellowshipped with God in:

R.A.Y.S.:

* **R**esting in His presence, **"casting all your anxiety on Him, because He cares for you" (1 Peter 5:7, NASB)**,

* **A**ppreciation of Him, even amidst hardship,

* **Y**oke with Christ of love toward others, and

* **S**itting at His feet to listen to His teaching.

~ Pray for your evening and tomorrow's schedule

*　　　　　*　　　　　*

~Morning 19~
The Fellowship of Praise

Lord, help us defend our prayer lives, for our fellowship with You is hindered by...

10. Valuing our enemies' opinions above our Creator
    - **"Yet you have forgotten the LORD, your Creator, the one who stretched out the sky like a canopy and laid the foundations of the earth. Will you remain in constant dread of human oppressors? Will you continue to fear the anger of your enemies? Where is their fury and anger now? It is gone!" (Isaiah 51:13, NLT).**
11. Doubting instead of trusting in God's proven character
    - **"But he must ask in faith without any doubting, for the one who doubts is like the surf of the sea, driven and tossed by the wind" (James 1:6, NASB).**

How do these verses describe fellowship with darkness or fellowship with God?

_____

_____

_____

_____

_____

_____
_____
_____

Talk to God about your struggles in these areas.

_____
_____
_____
_____
_____
_____

Seek strength from God to fellowship with Him. **"If anyone serves, they should do so with the strength God provides, so that in all things God may be praised through Jesus Christ. To him be the glory and the power for ever and ever. Amen" (1 Peter 4:11b, NIV).**

_____
_____
_____
_____
_____
_____

Jesus, we draw near to You. You said,

"I am the resurrection and the life. Anyone who believes in me will live, even after dying. Everyone who lives in me and believes in me will never ever die" (John 11:25, NLT).

1) Daily prayers & prayer for today's schedule

2) Believers *(Names beginning with the letter 'T')*

-
-
-
-
-
-
-
-
-

3) Unbelievers & People Groups

-
-
-
-
-
-

Relational Vision & Strategy 10 ~ Listening to Christ

What are your goals, struggles, and successes in listening to the Word of God? How are these goals being scheduled? (See "Day 29" for a sample Bible study method).

- **Goals**
-
-
-
-
- **Struggles**
-
-
-
- **Successes**
-
-
-
-

Talk to God about your goals and struggles. Rejoice and thank God for your growth and successes!

~Evening 19~

~ Write in your calendar how you fellowshipped with God in:

R.A.Y.S.:

* **R**esting in His presence, **"casting all your anxiety on Him, because He cares for you" (1 Peter 5:7, NASB)**,

* **A**ppreciation of Him, even amidst hardship,

* **Y**oke with Christ of love toward others, and

* **S**itting at His feet to listen to His teaching.

~ Pray for your evening and tomorrow's schedule

*   *   *

~Morning 20~
The Fellowship of Praise

Lord, help us defend our prayer lives, for our fellowship with You is hindered by...

12. Complaining when serving God
    - "...serve the LORD your God with joy and enthusiasm for the abundant benefits you have received" (Deuteronomy 28:47b, NLT).
    - "If you do not [serve God in this way]...you will serve your enemies whom the LORD will send against you..." (Deuteronomy 28:47a, 48a NLT).
13. Devaluing Christ, viewing Him as commonplace
    - "Again the Kingdom of Heaven is like a merchant looking for fine pearls. When he found one of great value, he went away and sold everything he had and bought it" (Matthew 13:45, 46, NIV).

How do these verses describe fellowship with darkness or fellowship with God?

_____

_____

_____

_____

_____

_____

_____

_____

Talk to God about your struggles in these areas.

_____

_____

_____

_____

_____

_____

Seek strength from God to fellowship with Him. **"If anyone serves, they should do so with the strength God provides, so that in all things God may be praised through Jesus Christ. To him be the glory and the power for ever and ever. Amen" (1 Peter 4:11b, NIV).**

_____

_____

_____

_____

_____

_____

Father, we come to You through Jesus. He said,

"I am the way, the truth, and the life. No one can come to the Father except through me" (John 14:6, NLT).

1) Daily prayers & prayer for today's schedule

2) Believers *(Names beginning with the letter 'U & V')*

-
-
-
-
-
-
-
-
-

3) Unbelievers & People Groups

-
-
-
-
-
-

Level Zero Groups: Maldives – New Caledonia

"And this gospel of the kingdom will be preached in the whole world as a testimony to all nations, and then the end will come" (Matthew 24:14, NIV).

Maldives	Deaf Maldivans	1833
Mali	Bangi Me	2420
Mali	Dogon Kolum So	35136
Malta	Deaf Maltese	1960
Mauritania	Deaf Mauritanians	6208
Mauritania	Zenaga	7841
Micronesia	Carolinian	2948
Micronesia	Namonuito	966
Micronesia	Ngatik	608
Micronesia	Satawalese	499
Mongolia	Deaf Mongolians	13745
Morocco	Deaf Moroccans	156060
Mozambique	Deaf Mozambicans	91681
Myanmar	Deaf Myanmarese	259132
Nepal	Byangsi	5670
Nepal	Chhulung	1634
Nepal	Deaf Nepalese	160033
Nepal	Ghale, Northern	2050
Nepal	Jerung	2427
Nepal	Kutang Bhotia	1932
Nepal	Lumba-Yakkha	1518
Nepal	Nar-Phuba	590
Nepal	Thudam Bhotia	2283
Nepal	Tilung	385

Nepal	Tseku	6075
Netherlands Antilles	Deaf Dutch Antilleans	1094
New Caledonia	Ara	472
New Caledonia	Aragure	1596
New Caledonia	Aro	923
New Caledonia	Dubea	2354
New Caledonia	Fwai	1681
New Caledonia	Hameha	506
New Caledonia	Javanese	10893
New Caledonia	Kaldosh Euronesian	1218
New Caledonia	Kwenyi	3023
New Caledonia	Neku	336
New Caledonia	Nemi	1008
New Caledonia	Nyua-Bonde	2865
New Caledonia	Pinje	168
New Caledonia	Sirhe	51
New Caledonia	Tiri	1008
New Caledonia	West Uvean	3142
New Caledonia	Xaracuu	5881

~Evening 20~

~ Write in your calendar how you fellowshipped with God in:

R.A.Y.S.:

* **R**esting in His presence, **"casting all your anxiety on Him, because He cares for you" (1 Peter 5:7, NASB)**,

* **A**ppreciation of Him, even amidst hardship,

* **Y**oke with Christ of love toward others, and

* **S**itting at His feet to listen to His teaching.

~ Pray for your evening and tomorrow's schedule

*   *   *

~Morning 21~
The Fellowship of Praise

Lord, help us defend our prayer lives, for our fellowship with You is hindered by...

14. Not sharing God's mercy in order to safeguard one's own life
    - **"Because thy lovingkindness is better than life, my lips shall praise thee" (Psalm 63:3, KJV).**
15. Valuing family above God
    - **"For God so loved the world that he gave his one and only Son..." (John 3:16a, NIV).**
16. Valuing money above God
    - **"'Bring one-tenth of your income into the storehouse so that there may be food in my house. Test me in this way,' says the LORD of Armies. 'See if I won't open the windows of heaven for you and flood you with blessings'" (Malachi 3:10, GWT).**

How do these verses describe fellowship with darkness or fellowship with God?

_____

_____

_____

_____

_____

_____

_____

_____

Talk to God about your struggles in these areas.

_____

_____

_____

_____

_____

_____

Seek strength from God to fellowship with Him. **"If anyone serves, they should do so with the strength God provides, so that in all things God may be praised through Jesus Christ. To him be the glory and the power for ever and ever. Amen" (1 Peter 4:11b, NIV).**

_____

_____

_____

_____

_____

_____

Jesus, we draw near to You. You said,

"Yes, I am the vine; you are the branches. Those who remain in me, and I in them, will produce much fruit. For apart from me you can do nothing" **(John 15:5, NLT).**

1) Daily prayers & prayer for today's schedule

2) Believers *(Names beginning with the letter 'W & X')*

-
-
-
-
-
-
-
-
-

3) Unbelievers & People Groups

-
-
-
-
-

Relational Vision & Strategy 11 ~ Sharing Christ with Others

What are your goals, struggles, and successes in these relationships? How are these goals being scheduled? (See "Day 30" for a sample way of sharing the Gospel).

- **Goals**
-
-
-
-

- **Struggles**
-
-
-
-

- **Successes**
-
-
-
-

Talk to God about your goals and struggles. Rejoice and thank God for your growth and successes!

~Evening 21~

~ Write in your calendar how you fellowshipped with God in:

R.A.Y.S.:

* **R**esting in His presence, **"casting all your anxiety on Him, because He cares for you" (1 Peter 5:7, NASB)**,

* **A**ppreciation of Him, even amidst hardship,

* **Y**oke with Christ of love toward others, and

* **S**itting at His feet to listen to His teaching.

~ Pray for your evening and tomorrow's schedule

*   *   *

PRAYER PLATOON DISCUSSION 4:

Part I. Review the War Plan for Praising our Beloved Savior and King

To praise and thank God, even amidst hardship, is to put on **"the hope of salvation as a helmet" (1 Thessalonians 5:8, NIV)** in your war to abide in Christ.

1) Which verses from the past week have helped you in your prayer life? Which verses challenge you?

_____

_____

_____

Regarding fellowshipping with God in **R.A.Y.S.**, did you have a Green, Yellow, or Red week?

_____

_____

_____

2) What are some personal activities you can do to praise and appreciate God?

_____

_____

_____

The following are some suggestions for improving your relationships with others:

    i.   **Set aside a time to write (or think about) what you are thankful for. Perhaps you can pair this with a second cup of coffee in the afternoon.**

    ii.   **Find a time to sing praises to God. Experiment with various formats of praise, such as listening to a CD, singing with a hymnal, etc.**

    iii.   **Take the Lord's Supper with others regularly.**

Remember the promise Christ taught us about rejoicing. He said, **"Blessed are you when men cast insults at you, and persecute you, and say all kinds of evil against you falsely on account of me. Rejoice, and be glad, for your reward in heaven is great, for so they persecuted the prophets who were before you" (Matthew 5:11, 12, NASB 1977).** Protect your relationship with Christ through praising God amidst any circumstance.

Part II. Introduction to Prayer Battleground Four: *The Fellowship of Leaning on our Beloved Savior and King*

3) On a scale of 1 to 10, with 10 being the highest, how much do you lean on God amidst your anxieties and problems?

_____

_____

_____

Memory Verse
"Who is this coming up from the wilderness leaning on her beloved?" (Song of Solomon 8:5a, NIV).

Introduction: The Warfare Against Leaning on our Beloved Savior and King

4) What hardships cause you to worry most?

_____

_____

_____

Christ taught, **"I am the vine; you are the branches. If you remain in me and I in you, you will bear much fruit; apart from me you can do nothing" (John 15:5, NIV)**. Thus, the time you spend leaning on Christ amidst hardship is the center of your prayer life. The Spirit of God fellowships with us in leaning on Christ. It is written of Christ's bride, **"The Spirit and the bride say, 'Come!'" (Revelation 22:17a, NIV)**.

5) What are the obstacles in your life to leaning on Christ?

_____

_____

_____

Satan, in order to block your way of abiding in Christ, desires to keep you in bondage to <u>neglecting your relationship with Christ</u>, that you might not bear fruit. Some of following verses illustrate bondage to <u>forms of neglecting your relationship with Christ</u>, which hinders our prayers. Others of the following verses demonstrate how to abide in Christ through vigilantly leaning on Him. Take time to reflect on these verses daily so that you can defend your prayer life.

*　　　*　　　*

~Morning 22~
The Fellowship of Leaning on Christ

Lord, help us defend our prayer lives, for our fellowship with You is hindered by...

1) Viewing prayer as a duty rather than a relationship of love
   - **"But I have this complaint against you. You don't love me or each other as you did at first" (Revelation 2:4, NLT).**
   - **"But I am afraid that just as Eve was deceived by the serpent's cunning, your minds may somehow be led astray from your sincere and pure devotion to Christ" (2 Corinthians 11:3, NIV).**
2) Preferring worldliness rather than Christ's presence
   - [Jesus said,] **"Look! I stand at the door and knock. If you hear my voice and open the door, I will come in, and we will share a meal together as friends" (Revelation 3:20, NLT).**
   - **"You will seek me and find me when you seek me with all your heart" (Jeremiah 29:13, NIV).**

How do these verses describe fellowship with darkness or fellowship with God?

_____

_____

_____

_____

_____

_____

_____

_____

Talk to God about your struggles in these areas.

_____

_____

_____

_____

_____

_____

Seek strength from God to fellowship with Him. **"If anyone serves, they should do so with the strength God provides, so that in all things God may be praised through Jesus Christ. To him be the glory and the power for ever and ever. Amen" (1 Peter 4:11b, NIV).**

_____

_____

_____

_____

_____

_____

Jesus, we draw near to You. You said,

"I am the bread of life. Whoever comes to me will never be hungry again. Whoever believes in me will never be thirsty" (John 6:35, NLT).

1) Daily prayers & prayer for today's schedule

2) Believers *(Names beginning with the letter 'Y & Z')*

-
-
-
-
-
-
-
-
-

3) Unbelievers & People Groups

-
-
-
-
-
-
-

Level Zero Groups: New Caledonia – Russia

"…repentance and forgiveness of sins should be proclaimed in his name to all nations, beginning from Jerusalem" (Luke 24:47, ESV).

New Caledonia	Yalayu	2119
Nigeria	Baangi	19404
Nigeria	Deaf Nigerians	742699
Nigeria	Dulbu	338
Nigeria	Kamkam	5520
Nigeria	Kyangawa	21224
Nigeria	Maha	26498
Nigeria	Shani	563
Nigeria	Taura	4416
North Korea	Deaf North Koreans	113136
Norway	Deaf Norwegians	21927
Oman	Batahira	1194
Oman	Deaf Omanis	15614
Oman	Harsusi	1384
Oman	Hobyot	138
Oman	Jibbali	41321
Oman	Kumzari	4959
Oman	Luwati	15000
Pakistan	Deaf Pakistanis	29302
Pakistan	Dumaki	1290
Pakistan	Gowro	300
Pakistan	Lassi	13804
Pakistan	Rajkoti	19720

Pakistan	Ushojo	3037
Pakistan	Yidgha	6000
Panama	Deaf Panamanians	18087
Papua New Guinea	Deaf Papua New Guineans	25598
Paraguay	Emok	1300
Paraguay	Mataco	2600
Peru	Deaf Peruvians	144183
Peru	Isconahua	90
Peru	Mashco Piro	103
Portugal	Deaf Portuguese	50717
Portugal	Mirandesa	10000
Qatar	Deaf Qataris	4495
Russia	Akhwakh	6500
Russia	Archi	2000
Russia	Bagvalal	6500
Russia	Chamalal	9500
Russia	Ginukh	200
Russia	Godoberi	2900
Russia	Hunzib	2000

~Evening 22~

~ Write in your calendar how you fellowshipped with God in:

R.A.Y.S.:

* **R**esting in His presence, **"casting all your anxiety on Him, because He cares for you" (1 Peter 5:7, NASB)**,

* **A**ppreciation of Him, even amidst hardship,

* **Y**oke with Christ of love toward others, and

* **S**itting at His feet to listen to His teaching.

~ Pray for your evening and tomorrow's schedule

*   *   *

~Morning 23~
The Fellowship of Leaning on Christ

Lord, help us defend our prayer lives, for our fellowship with You is hindered by...

3) Being a religious actor rather than Christ's dear friend

- [Jesus said,] **"On judgment day, many will say to me, 'Lord! Lord! We prophesied in your name and cast out demons in your name and performed many miracles in your name.' But I will reply, 'I never knew you. Get away from me, you who break God's law'"** (Matthew 7:22, 23, NLT).

4) Choosing to be proud instead of being humble

- [God says,] **"...I live in the high and holy place with those whose spirits are contrite and humble"** (Isaiah 57:15b, NLT).

- **"Then if my people who are called by my name will humble themselves and pray and seek my face and turn from their wicked ways, I will hear from heaven and will forgive their sins and restore their land"** (2 Chronicles 7:14, NLT).

How do these verses describe fellowship with darkness or fellowship with God?

_____

_____

_____

_____

_____

_____

_____

_____

Talk to God about your struggles in these areas.

_____

_____

_____

_____

_____

_____

Seek strength from God to fellowship with Him. **"If anyone serves, they should do so with the strength God provides, so that in all things God may be praised through Jesus Christ. To him be the glory and the power for ever and ever. Amen" (1 Peter 4:11b, NIV).**

_____

_____

_____

_____

_____

_____

Jesus, we draw near to You. You said,

"I am the light of the world. He who follows Me shall not walk in darkness, but have the light of life" (John 8:12, NKJV).

1) Daily prayers & prayer for today's schedule

2) Believers *(Names of Government/Military Leaders, 1 Tim. 2:2)*

-
-
-
-
-
-
-
-
-

3) Unbelievers & People Groups

-
-
-
-
-
-

Relational Vision & Strategy 12 ~ Thanksgiving

What are your goals, struggles, and successes in this area? How are these goals being scheduled?

- **Goals**
-
-
-
-
- **Struggles**
-
-
-
- **Successes**
-
-
-
-

Talk to God about your goals and struggles. Rejoice and thank God for your growth and successes!

~Evening 23~

~ Write in your calendar how you fellowshipped with God in:

R.A.Y.S.:

* **R**esting in His presence, **"casting all your anxiety on Him, because He cares for you" (1 Peter 5:7, NASB)**,

* **A**ppreciation of Him, even amidst hardship,

* **Y**oke with Christ of love toward others, and

* **S**itting at His feet to listen to His teaching.

~ Pray for your evening and tomorrow's schedule

*   *   *

~Morning 24~
The Fellowship of Leaning on Christ

Lord, help us defend our prayer lives, for our fellowship with You is hindered by...

5) Worry (King Hezekiah modeled for us a path of leaning on God in the midst of his people being threatened.)
   - **"After Hezekiah received the [threatening] letter from the messengers and read it, he went up to the Lord's temple and spread it out before the LORD" (Isaiah 37:14, NLT).**
6) Not being still
   - **"He says, 'Be still and know that I am God; I will be exalted among the nations, I will be exalted in the earth'" (Psalm 46:10, NLT).**

How do these verses describe fellowship with darkness or fellowship with God?

_____
_____
_____
_____
_____
_____
_____
_____

Talk to God about your struggles in these areas.

_____

_____

_____

_____

_____

_____

Seek strength from God to fellowship with Him. **"If anyone serves, they should do so with the strength God provides, so that in all things God may be praised through Jesus Christ. To him be the glory and the power for ever and ever. Amen" (1 Peter 4:11b, NIV).**

_____

_____

_____

_____

_____

_____

Jesus, we draw near to You. You said,

"Yes, I am the gate. Those who come in through me will be saved. They will come and go freely and will find good pastures" (John 10:9, NLT).

1) Daily prayers & prayer for today's schedule

2) Believers *(Names of Prisoners, Hebrews 13:3)*

-
-
-
-
-
-
-
-
-
-

3) Unbelievers & People Groups

-
-
-
-
-
-

Level Zero Groups: Russia – Sudan

"But my life is worth nothing to me unless I use it for finishing the work assigned me by the Lord Jesus--the work of telling others the Good News about the wonderful grace of God" (Acts 20:24, NLT).

Russia	Karata	5000
Russia	Khwarshi	1000
Russia	Tindi	5000
Russia	Tsez	7000
Rwanda	Deaf Rwandans	41162
Samoa	Deaf Samoans	860
San Marino	Emiliano-Romagnolo	22889
Saudi Arabia	Deaf Saudi Arabians	146436
Saudi Arabia	Shahara	43120
Senegal	Deaf Senegalese	65786
Serbia	Deaf Serbians	47457
Singapore	Deaf Singaporeans	22742
Slovenia	Deaf Slovenians	9799
Solomon Is.	Deaf Solomon Islanders	2503
Somalia	Dabarre	33057
Somalia	Deaf Somalis	47773
Somalia	Garre	82642
Somalia	Jiiddu	28515
Somalia	Mushungulu	28515
Somalia	Tunni	33057
South Sudan	Adja	291

South Sudan	Atwot	65974
South Sudan	Banda-Banda	4061
South Sudan	Banda-Mbres	10836
South Sudan	Banda-Ndele	22693
South Sudan	Bari Bai	3501
South Sudan	Dongotono	1061
South Sudan	Indri	980
South Sudan	Lango	41955
South Sudan	Lopit	70012
South Sudan	Ngalgulgule	1211
South Sudan	Thuri	20006
Spain	Fala	10500
Sri Lanka	Deaf Sri Lankans	87271
St. Lucia	Deaf Saint Lucians	812
Sudan	Baygo	1960
Sudan	Binga	1400
Sudan	Dair	1400
Sudan	Dar Fur Daju	98017
Sudan	Deaf Sudanese	214848
Sudan	Dgik	81289
Sudan	El Hugeirat	1428

~Evening 24~

~ Write in your calendar how you fellowshipped with God in:

R.A.Y.S.:

* **R**esting in His presence, **"casting all your anxiety on Him, because He cares for you" (1 Peter 5:7, NASB)**,

* **A**ppreciation of Him, even amidst hardship,

* **Y**oke with Christ of love toward others, and

* **S**itting at His feet to listen to His teaching.

~ Pray for your evening and tomorrow's schedule

*   *   *

~Morning 25~
The Fellowship of Leaning on Christ

Lord, help us defend our prayer lives, for our fellowship with You is hindered by...

7) Not seeking God for help
   - **"You do not have because you do not ask God" (James 4:2b, NLT).**

8) Not caring to pray for the needs of others
   - **"And so, from the day we heard, we have not ceased to pray for you..." (Colossians 1:9a, ESV).**

How do these verses describe fellowship with darkness or fellowship with God?

_____

_____

_____

_____

_____

_____

_____

_____

Talk to God about your struggles in these areas.

_____

_____

_____

_____

_____

_____

Seek strength from God to fellowship with Him. **"If anyone serves, they should do so with the strength God provides, so that in all things God may be praised through Jesus Christ. To him be the glory and the power for ever and ever. Amen" (1 Peter 4:11b, NIV).**

_____

_____

_____

_____

_____

_____

Jesus, we draw near to You. You said,

"I am the good shepherd. The good shepherd sacrifices his life for the sheep" (John 10:11, NLT).

1) Daily prayers & prayer for today's schedule

2) Believers *(Distressed Neighbors, James 1:27)*

-
-
-
-
-
-
-
-
-
-

3) Unbelievers & People Groups

-
-
-
-
-
-
-

Relational Vision & Strategy 13 ~ Worshiping God Together

What are your goals, struggles, and successes in this area? How are these goals being scheduled?

- **Goals**
-
-
-
-
- **Struggles**
-
-
-
- **Successes**
-
-
-
-

Talk to God about your goals and struggles. Rejoice and thank God for your growth and successes!

~Evening 25~

~ Write in your calendar how you fellowshipped with God in:

R.A.Y.S.:

* **R**esting in His presence, **"casting all your anxiety on Him, because He cares for you" (1 Peter 5:7, NASB)**,

* **A**ppreciation of Him, even amidst hardship,

* **Y**oke with Christ of love toward others, and

* **S**itting at His feet to listen to His teaching.

~ Pray for your evening and tomorrow's schedule

*　　　　*　　　　*

~Morning 26~
The Fellowship of Leaning on Christ

Lord, help us defend our prayer lives, for our fellowship with You is hindered by...

9) Refusing to pray together with others
   - **"For where two or three are gathered together in my name, there am I in the midst of them" (Matthew 18:20, KJV).**

10) Avoiding praying with diverse groups of believers
    - **"They all joined together constantly in prayer, along with the women and Mary the mother of Jesus, and with his brothers" (Acts 1:14, NIV).**

How do these verses describe fellowship with darkness or fellowship with God?

_____
_____
_____
_____
_____
_____
_____
_____
_____

Talk to God about your struggles in these areas.

_____

_____

_____

_____

_____

_____

Seek strength from God to fellowship with Him. **"If anyone serves, they should do so with the strength God provides, so that in all things God may be praised through Jesus Christ. To him be the glory and the power for ever and ever. Amen" (1 Peter 4:11b, NIV).**

_____

_____

_____

_____

_____

_____

Jesus, we draw near to You. You said,

"I am the resurrection and the life. Anyone who believes in me will live, even after dying. Everyone who lives in me and believes in me will never ever die" (John 11:25, NLT).

1) Daily prayers & prayer for today's schedule

2) Believers *(Names of Church Leaders, 2 Cor. 1:11)*

-
-
-
-
-
-
-
-
-
-
-
-
-
-
-
-
-
-

Level Zero Groups: Sudan – Tanzania

"And they sang a new song, saying: 'You are worthy to take the scroll and to open its seals, because you were slain, and with your blood you purchased for God persons from every tribe and language and people and nation'" (Revelation 5:9, NIV).

Sudan	Eliri	4919
Sudan	Fa-c-Aka	3903
Sudan	Fanya	48394
Sudan	Fertit	11589
Sudan	Fongoro	1294
Sudan	Fungor	3757
Sudan	Ingessana	97802
Sudan	Kamdang	4201
Sudan	Kanga	12682
Sudan	Kara	280
Sudan	Karko	18547
Sudan	Keiga	17906
Sudan	Keiga Jirru	1960
Sudan	Kufa-Lima	15219
Sudan	Lafofa	7197
Sudan	Logol	3641
Sudan	Masakin	48193
Sudan	Midob	72841
Sudan	Mima	100940
Sudan	Molo	140
Sudan	Tagale	114704
Sudan	Tagoy	18567
Sudan	Talodi	2100

Sudan	Tese	1960
Sudan	Tima	1571
Sudan	Tingal	10982
Sudan	Togole	45324
Sudan	Tulishi	11615
Sudan	Tumale	2200
Sudan	Tumtum	10426
Sudan	Wali	1346
Sudan	Wali	52775
Sudan	Warnang	1571
Sudan	Yulu	4922
Suriname	Deaf Surinamers	2484
Swaziland	Deaf Swazis	6080
Sweden	Ingrian-Finns	300
Sweden	Swedish Travellers	25000
Sweden	Tattare Gypsies	25000
Switzerland	Deaf Swiss	38540
Syria	Deaf Syrians	104847
Syria	Lomavren	466180
Tajikistan	Aimaq	7762
Tajikistan	Parya	3000
Tanzania	Deaf Tanzanians	232722
Tanzania	Ndonde	17687

~Evening 26~

~ Write in your calendar how you fellowshipped with God in:

R.A.Y.S.:

* **R**esting in His presence, **"casting all your anxiety on Him, because He cares for you" (1 Peter 5:7, NASB)**,

* **A**ppreciation of Him, even amidst hardship,

* **Y**oke with Christ of love toward others, and

* **S**itting at His feet to listen to His teaching.

~ Pray for your evening and tomorrow's schedule

*　　　　*　　　　*

~Morning 27~
The Fellowship of Leaning on Christ

Lord, help us defend our prayer lives, for our fellowship with You is hindered by...

11) Fasting in order to be seen by others rather than to focus on God

- **"When you fast, do not look somber as the hypocrites do for they disfigure their faces to show others they are fasting. Truly, I tell you, they have received their reward in full. But when you fast, put oil on your head and wash your face" (Matthew 6:16, 17, NLT).**

12) Avoiding fasting for church leaders

- **"So when they had appointed elders in every church, and prayed with fasting, they commended them to the Lord in whom they had believed" (Acts 14:23, ESV).**

How do these verses describe fellowship with darkness or fellowship with God?

_____

_____

_____

_____

_____

_____

_____

_____

Talk to God about your struggles in these areas.

_____

_____

_____

_____

_____

_____

Seek strength from God to fellowship with Him. **"If anyone serves, they should do so with the strength God provides, so that in all things God may be praised through Jesus Christ. To him be the glory and the power for ever and ever. Amen" (1 Peter 4:11b, NIV).**

_____

_____

_____

_____

_____

_____

Father, we come to You through Jesus. He said,

"I am the way, the truth, and the life. No one can come to the Father except through me" (John 14:6, NLT).

1) Daily prayers & prayer for today's schedule

2) Believers *(Local Outreach Leaders, 2 Thess. 3:1)*

-
-
-
-
-
-
-
-
-
-
-
-
-
-
-
-
-
-

Relational Vision & Strategy 14 ~ "Add lavishly to your faith heroic deeds..."[2] (2 Peter 1:5a)

As we are yoked with Christ, who lived heroically, we are called to live heroically. What are your goals, struggles, and successes in this area? How are these goals being scheduled?

- **Goals**
-
-
-

- **Struggles**
-
-
-

- **Successes**
-
-

Talk to God about your goals and struggles. Rejoice and thank God for your growth and successes!

---

[2] My translation is based on MacArthur's note, "'Add' is to give lavishly and generously... First in Peter's list of moral excellencies is a word that, in classical Gr., meant the God-given ability to perform heroic deeds..." John MacArthur, ed., *The MacArthur Study Bible* (Nashville: Thomas Nelson Publishers, 1997), note on 2 Peter 1:5.

~Evening 27~

~ Write in your calendar how you fellowshipped with God in:

R.A.Y.S.:

* **R**esting in His presence, **"casting all your anxiety on Him, because He cares for you" (1 Peter 5:7, NASB)**,

* **A**ppreciation of Him, even amidst hardship,

* **Y**oke with Christ of love toward others, and

* **S**itting at His feet to listen to His teaching.

~ Pray for your evening and tomorrow's schedule

*   *   *

~Morning 28~
The Fellowship of Leaning on Christ

Lord, help us defend our prayer lives, for our fellowship with You is hindered by...

13) Avoiding fasting for missionaries
- **"While they were worshiping the Lord and fasting, the Holy Spirit said, 'Set apart for me Barnabus and Saul for the work to which I have called them'" (Acts 13:2, NIV).**

14) Avoiding a fast which focuses on helping the poor and oppressed
- **"If you spend yourself in behalf of the hungry and satisfy the needs of the oppressed, then your light will rise in the darkness, and your night will become like the noonday" (Isaiah 58:10, NIV).**

How do these verses describe fellowship with darkness or fellowship with God?

_____
_____
_____
_____
_____
_____
_____
_____

Talk to God about your struggles in these areas.

_____

_____

_____

_____

_____

_____

Seek strength from God to fellowship with Him. **"If anyone serves, they should do so with the strength God provides, so that in all things God may be praised through Jesus Christ. To him be the glory and the power for ever and ever. Amen" (1 Peter 4:11b, NIV).**

_____

_____

_____

_____

_____

_____

Jesus, we draw near to You. You said,

"Yes, I am the vine; you are the branches. Those who remain in me, and I in them, will produce much fruit. For apart from me you can do nothing" *(John 15:5, NLT).*

1) Daily prayers & prayer for today's schedule

2) Believers *(Global Outreach Leaders, Ephesians 6:19)*

-
-
-
-
-
-
-
-
-
-
-
-
-
-
-
-

Level Zero Groups: Tanzania – Zambia

"For the Lord gave us this command when he said, 'I have made you a light to the Gentiles, to bring salvation to the farthest corners of the earth'" (Acts 13:47, NLT).

Tanzania	Pimbwe	51744
Tanzania	Segeju	18360
Tanzania	Vinza	19380
The Bahamas	Deaf Bahamians	1562
The Gambia	Deaf Gambians	9005
Timor Leste	Adabe	1294
Timor Leste	Kairui-Midik	2000
Timor Leste	Waimaha	5968
Tunisia	Deaf Tunisians	51887
Tunisia	Ghadames	2978
Tunisia	Tmagourt	7122
Uganda	Mening	6462
Uganda	Nubian	24965
United Arab Emirates	Deaf Emirians	17467
United Kingdom	Parsee	75000
United Kingdom	Scottish Travellers	4000
United States	Brunei	699
United States	Khuen	3042
United States	Mokilese	466
Vanuatu	Aore	13
Vanuatu	Deaf Ni-Vanuatuans	1318

Vanuatu	Vao	2519
Vanuatu	Wusi-Kerepua	402
Venezuela	Mandahuaca	3000
Venezuela	Mapoyo	365
Vietnam	Chut	6022
Vietnam	Gelao	2100
Vietnam	Pubiao	687
Vietnam	Red Tai	163340
Vietnam	Romam	436
Vietnam	Sila	709
Vietnam	Tsun-Lao	15396
West Bank	Deaf Palestinians	20699
West Bank	Samaritans	798
Yemen	Deaf Yemenis	97000
Yemen	Hobyot	29851
Zambia	Deaf Zambians	50047

~Evening 28~

~ Write in your calendar how you fellowshipped with God in:

R.A.Y.S.:

* **R**esting in His presence, **"casting all your anxiety on Him, because He cares for you" (1 Peter 5:7, NASB)**,

* **A**ppreciation of Him, even amidst hardship,

* **Y**oke with Christ of love toward others, and

* **S**itting at His feet to listen to His teaching.

~ Pray for your evening and tomorrow's schedule

*   *   *

Juice Day Notes

For the remainder of the month, take some time to fast (with the permission of your physician), schedule the events for the upcoming month, coordinate schedules with your household, and pray through your schedules together. If your children want to fast with you, consider having a "Juice Morning" to fast and pray together. Instruct them to write down the verses that God brings to mind.

_____
_____
_____
_____
_____
_____
_____
_____
_____
_____
_____
_____

PRAYER PLATOON DISCUSSION 5:

Part I. Review the War Plan for Leaning on our Beloved Savior and King

To lean on Christ is to take up **"the shield of faith"** **(Ephesians 6:16)** in your war to abide in Christ.

1) Which verses from the past week have helped you in your prayer life? Which verses challenge you?

_____

_____

_____

2) Regarding fellowshipping with God in **R.A.Y.S.**, did you have a Green, Yellow, or Red week?

_____

_____

_____

3) What are some personal activities you can do to lean on Christ?

_____

_____

_____

The following are some suggestions for leaning on God:

i. **Find a time to meet with God alone. Perhaps you can pair this with an early morning cup of coffee.**

ii. **Make every meeting with other believers into a prayer meeting. Perhaps you can plan to pray with them at the end of your time together.**

iii. **Find a time to have a fast from solid foods and have a "juice day". Perhaps this can be a couple of meals a week, when you need to make an important decision (see Acts 14:23), or when someone is sick (see Psalm 35:13).**

Be encouraged by the following verse: **"…[God] rewards those who earnestly seek him" (Hebrews 11:6, NIV).** I am persuaded that Jesus Himself is our reward. Protect your relationship with Christ through leaning on Him for everything.

Part II. Continue in Your Prayer Platoon or Start Another Prayer Platoon.

4) How have you benefitted by going through this study with others?

_____

_____

_____

5) Would you be willing to continue in this Prayer Platoon or with a prayer partner?

_____

_____

_____

6) Would you be willing to start a new Prayer Platoon?

_____

_____

_____

*   *   *

~Morning 29~
Scripture Reading Plan

Reflect upon and write out your 3-month Bible reading goals.

_____
_____
_____
_____
_____
_____
_____
_____
_____
_____
_____
_____

   To have a consistent morning Bible time, I pair a positive (coffee) with a negative (waking up early). I anchor my morning Bible reading with a good cup of coffee.

   Though you may have your own Bible study method, below is a three-step plan for reading the Bible:

Focus on Fellowship

Fellowship with God versus fellowship with darkness is perhaps the most important theme of the Scriptures.

Use the following passage to practice focusing on fellowship with God. In the passage above, <u>underline</u> verses that   describe fellowship with God (and the consequences thereof). <u>Draw bullet points</u> before and after verses ●...●that describe fellowship with darkness (or the consequences thereof).

> *"He commanded the Red Sea to dry up.*
> > *He led Israel across the sea as if it were a desert.*
>
> *So he rescued them from their enemies*
> > *and redeemed them from their foes.*
>
> *Then the water returned and covered their enemies;*
> > *not one of them survived.*
>
> *Then his people believed his promises.*
> > *Then they sang his praise.*
>
> *Yet how quickly they forgot what he had done!*
> > *They wouldn't wait for his counsel!*
>
> *In the wilderness their desires ran wild,*
> > *testing God's patience in that dry wasteland.*
>
> *So he gave them what they asked for,*
> > *but he sent a plague along with it.*
> *(Psalm 106: 9-15, NLT).*

Focus on Repentance

Reread the passage above and talk to God about your struggles in fellowshipping with Him in the ways the Scriptures describe. Seek strength from God to fellowship with Him **(1 Peter 4:11b, NIV).**

1) Focus on Retelling

Talk with one or two others about what you have discovered from your study about fellowship with God. Also, talk to them about your own struggles and successes in fellowshipping with God. Sharing with believers is excellent practice for sharing your faith with those who haven't heard the Gospel.

It is written, **"these are the things God has revealed to us by his Spirit. The Spirit searches all things, even the deep things of God" (1 Corinthians 2:11, NIV).** In these three steps, we deeply study the Word and fellowship with the Spirit of God.[3]

---

[3] Kenneth Wuest, *Word Studies: Untranslatable Riches of the Greek New Testament* (Grand Rapids: William B. Eerdmans, 1942), note on The Fellowship and Communion of the Holy Spirit.

~Evening 29~

~ Write in your calendar how you fellowshipped with God in:

R.A.Y.S.:

* **R**esting in His presence, **"casting all your anxiety on Him, because He cares for you" (1 Peter 5:7, NASB)**,

* **A**ppreciation of Him, even amidst hardship,

* **Y**oke with Christ of love toward others, and

* **S**itting at His feet to listen to His teaching.

~ Pray for your evening and tomorrow's schedule

      *   *   *

~Morning 30~
Practice Sharing the Gospel

Take time today to practice sharing the Gospel.

Though you may have your own evangelism method, below is "Creation to the New Creation" Gospel presentation using the acrostic WORD:

*　　*　　*

Creation to the New Creation

<u>W</u>ord: God created the universe with His speech, His infinite **"Word" (Psalm 33:6),** and by His **"Spirit" (Genesis 1:2; Psalm 33:6)**. He created, loved, and spent time with mankind. Then sin entered the world and messed everything up – our relationship with God and our relationships with one another were destroyed. So, after the time of Abraham and after the time of David, God sent His infinite Word again to redeem us.

Jesus is God's infinite "**Word**" that **"became flesh" (John 1:1-14)**. At Jesus' baptism, it says that **"...the Holy Spirit descended on him in bodily form like a dove..." (Luke 3:22a, NIV)**. Thus, God sent His Word and His Spirit again to start a **"new creation" (cf. Isaiah 57:17, 25 with Isaiah 11:1, 2, 6)**.

<u>O</u>ffering: Jesus said, "**I am the good shepherd. The good shepherd lays down his life for the sheep" (John 10:11, New International Version)**.

Some days before his death on a cross, Jesus was at a house with his disciples. "…**While he was eating, a woman came in with a beautiful alabaster jar of expensive perfume made from essence of nard. She broke open the jar and poured the perfume over his head. Some of those at the table were indignant. "Why waste such expensive perfume?" they asked.**

But Jesus replied, 'Leave her alone. Why criticize her for doing such a good thing to me? She has done what she could and has anointed my body for burial ahead of time'" (Mark 14:3a, 4, 6, 8, NLT).

<u>R</u>*isen*: Three days after dying as an offering of atonement for our sins, Jesus, the infinite Word of God, rose from the grave. He taught, **"I am the resurrection and the life. Anyone who believes in me will live, even after dying" (John 11:25, New Living Translation).** God has said, **"Behold, I am making all things new" (Revelation 21:5a, English Standard Version),** and **"Therefore, if anyone is in Christ, he is a new creation. The old has passed away; behold, the new has come" (2 Corinthians 5:17, English Standard Version).**

<u>D</u>*ecide*: So, if you believe that Jesus is the Word of God, that He was the perfect sacrifice to cover our sins, and that He rose again from the grave, then you can become a part of the new creation: the new life - eternal life. Do you want this new life? If your decision is yes, pray with me.

Lord, thank you for sending Jesus, Your eternal Word, to redeem us. Thank you that You didn't leave us in brokenness. You said, **"For God so loved the world** *that he gave his one and only Son, that whoever believes in him shall not perish but have eternal life"* (John 3:16, NIV).

Jesus, I believe in You, that You are the Son, the infinite *"Word of God"* that created me for fellowship.

I believe You are *"The Good Shepherd"* who is the perfect offering, the atoning sacrifice that covers each of my sins. I confess each of my sins to You and ask for forgiveness. Thank you for Your forgiveness for each of my sins.

I believe that You rose from the grave and are, *"the resurrection and the life."* Jesus, I believe Your promise that with You I, *"will live, even after dying."* Thank you for Your forgiveness and for giving me *"eternal life"* that I might fellowship with You forever.

Lord, thank you for the gift of Your Spirit that now *"dwells in"* me *(1 Corinthians 3:16b, English Standard Version)*, and who helps me to fellowship with you daily. Help me to love others as You have loved me. Help me to share Your message of hope with others. Amen.

~Evening 30~

~ Write in your calendar how you fellowshipped with God in:

R.A.Y.S.:

* **R**esting in His presence, **"casting all your anxiety on Him, because He cares for you" (1 Peter 5:7, NASB),**

* **A**ppreciation of Him, even amidst hardship,

* **Y**oke with Christ of love toward others, and

* **S**itting at His feet to listen to His teaching.

~ Pray for your evening and tomorrow's schedule

*   *   *

About the author:

Rev. William Hernandez serves with Healing Lamplight Pathway (a church plant with the Puget Sound Baptist Association) as Pastor and Prayer Advocate for Hidden and Hurting People Worldwide. He earned a bachelor's degree from UC Berkeley, a master's degree from Golden Gate Baptist Theological Seminary, and a doctorate from Trinity Theological Seminary. He and his wife and eight children serve in Europe, the Middle East, and North Africa.

Made in the USA
San Bernardino, CA
16 June 2017